NUTRITION of the TURKEY

By

MILTON L. SCOTT, Ph.D.
Professor of Nutrition Emeritus at Cornell University

1987

PUBLISHED BY
M. L. SCOTT OF ITHACA
*PO Box 4464
Ithaca, NY 14852*

TABLE OF CONTENTS

CHAPTER 1 7

    DEVELOPMENT OF THE TURKEY INDUSTRY 7

        MANAGEMENT AND NUTRITION OF THE MODERN TURKEY . . 8

            Evolution of Knowledge Concerning the Genetics, Disease Control, Management, and Nutrition of Market Turkeys 12

            Genetic Improvements 14

            Progress in Disease Control 16

            Improved Management Practices 16

            Adoption of artificial insemination 17

            Rearing the poults 18

            Rearing breeders 19

            Evolution of Our Knowledge of Turkey Nutrition . . 19

            Feeding the breeders 24

    REFERENCES 25

CHAPTER 2 28

    ENERGY, PROTEIN AND AMINO ACID REQUIREMENTS OF TURKEYS 28

        Energy values for turkeys 29

        Amino acid requirements of growing turkeys 30

        Possible amino acid imbalances 33

        Formulation of diets balanced in energy, protein and amino acids 33

        Examples of turkey dietary regimens formulated at least-cost to demonstrate the relationship between energy-protein concentration and economy of turkey production 33

        Energy, protein and amino acid requirements of breeding trukeys 72

Amino acid requirements of breeding turkeys . . .	74
REFERENCES	78
CHAPTER 3	83
MINERAL REQUIREMENTS OF TURKEYS	83
CALCIUM AND PHOSPHORUS	83
CALCIUM AND PHOSPHORUS FOR BREEDERS	88
Calculation of the calcium requirement	88
Phosphorus for breeders	89
SODIUM, POTASSIUM AND CHLORIDE.	89
Sodium	90
Chloride	90
Symptoms of Deficiency	90
Effects of excess salt	91
Potassium	91
Symptoms of deficiency	92
MAGNESIUM, IRON AND COPPER	92
Magnesium	92
Iron	93
Copper	93
High dietary levels of copper	94
MANGANESE	94
ZINC.	96
SELENIUM	96
Studies on the effects of using dietary levels of selenium somewhat in excess of requirements .	101
Selenium toxicity	101
IODINE	101

MOLYBDENUM	101
SUMMARY OF MINERAL REQUIREMENTS	102
REFERENCES	103
CHAPTER 4	108
VITAMIN REQUIREMENTS OF TURKEYS	108
THE FAT-SOLUBLE VITAMINS	108
<u>Vitamin A</u>	108
<u>Vitamin D</u>	110
<u>Vitamin E</u>	114
<u>Vitamin K</u>	115
<u>Effects of mycotoxins on utilization of fat-soluble vitamins</u>	116
THE WATER-SOLUBLE VITAMINS	116
<u>Thiamin</u>	117
<u>Riboflavin</u>	119
<u>Niacin</u>	120
<u>Pantothenic acid</u>	121
<u>Biotin</u>	123
<u>Pyridoxine</u>	125
<u>Folic acid</u>	126
<u>Vitamin B_{12}</u>	128
<u>Choline</u>	128
SUMMARY OF THE VITAMINS IN TURKEY NUTRITION	129
REFERENCES	131
CHAPTER 5	137
ESSENTIAL FATTY ACIDS, UNIDENTIFIED FACTORS AND ANTIBIOTICS	137

UNIDENTIFIED FACTORS IN TURKEY NUTRITION 139

    Possible need for linolenic acid (omega-3 fatty acids) 139

    Possible unidentified factor/factors in fish solubles 139

    The grass juice factor 141

ANTIBIOTICS AND CHEMOTHERAPEAUTIC AGENTS AS GROWTH FACTORS 141

    Copper sulfate and the grass juice factor 142

SUMMARY REGARDING ESSENTIAL FATTY ACIDS, UNIDENTIFIED FACTORS AND ANTIBIOTICS FOR TURKEYS . . 142

REFERENCES 143

CHAPTER 6 146

    LEG WEAKNESSES, ASCITES, PENDULOUS CROPS, AORTIC RUPTURE AND OTHER ANOMALIES OF TURKEYS 146

    Leg weaknesses 146

    Unidentified factor in brewer's yeast 150

    Breast blisters 151

    Pendulous crops 152

    Usual cause of pendulous crops 152

    Foot pad dermatitis 152

    Tongue deformity 153

    Ascites 153

    Aortic rupture 154

REFERENCES 158

CHAPTER 7 162

FEEDS AND FEEDING OF TURKEYS 162

    Nutrient composition of feedstuffs for turkeys . . 162

    Research on "alternate" cereal grains for turkeys 162

Wheat	163
Barley	164
Millet	165
Triticale	165
CARBOHYDRATE SOURCES TO BE AVOIDED IN FEEDING TURKEYS	166
Cassava (also known as Manioc, Yuca, or Tapioca)	166
Rye	166
ALTERNATE PROTEIN SOURCES	166
Meat and bone meal	167
Fish meal	168
Rapeseed	169
BY-PRODUCTS OF WHEAT AND CORN MILLING	169
Wheat middlings, wheat millrun, wheat screenings and wheat bran	169
Corn gluten meal and corn gluten feed	169
FERMENTATION BY-PRODUCTS	170
Brewers' dried grains, corn distillers' dried grains with solubles, dried brewers' yeast and corn fermentation solubles	170
PRINCIPLES OF FEEDS AND FEEDING OF TURKEYS	170
REFERENCES	172

PREFACE

The turkey industry has grown rapidly during the past decade. Although a considerable amount of research has now been undertaken in turkey nutrition, no one has reviewed this research and presented it in a form useful to students, teachers, feed manufacturers and turkey producers.

Because the book, "Nutrition of the Chicken" by the author together with Nesheim and Young contains the basic nutritional information needed, but does not deal with the special problems of turkey nutrition, it was considered desirable to write a separate book on NUTRITION OF THE TURKEY.

This book presents the research and knowledge responsible for the Development of the Turkey Industry (Chapter 1); the Energy, Protein and Amino Acid Requirements of Turkeys (Chapter 2); the Mineral Requirements (Chapter 3); the Vitamin Requirements (Chapter 4); knowledge concerning the Essential Fatty Acids, Unidentified Factors, and Antibiotics in turkey nutrition (Chapter 5); Chapter 6 deals with leg weaknesses and other anomalies related to the nutrition of turkeys; and Chapter 7 discusses the Feeds and Feeding of Turkeys.

The author spent much of his professional career at Cornell University working and writing in turkey nutrition. This book represents an effort to present in writing a review of all of the research conducted in this area of nutrition and to indicate how this information may be best used for the most economical production of turkeys.

The author wishes to thank Ms Grace I. Saroka, Ms June M. Kopald and Mr James M. Saroka for their help in editing and preparation of the manuscript; and Ms. Paula Bensadoun for her art work.

M. L. Scott
Ithaca, N. Y.
September, 1987

CHAPTER 1

DEVELOPMENT OF THE TURKEY INDUSTRY

Although the origin of the turkey is shrouded in antiquity it is well known to be as American as the American Indian. Turkey bones have been found in Indian burial mounds in Tennessee, Kentucky and some other parts of the Southern United States. It is clear that the turkey served as food for the Indians as early as 1000 A. D., and perhaps earlier.

There is some evidence that turkeys were brought from Mexico back to Spain as early as 1498, but the first important transport of turkeys to Spain was carried out by some of the Spanish conquistadors in 1519-1520. From Spain the turkeys apparently spread over Europe and the Near East. They appear to have been introduced into England between 1524 and 1541 where they were highly sought after for gourmet dinners. In 1541, the Archbishop Cramer prohibited the appearance at State festivals of more than one dish of turkey cocks; the females were considered too precious to be cooked at all.

It was this intense interest in gourmet foods that was responsible for the importation by England of many new species of fowl for special repasts. Guinea fowls were imported from Africa via Turkey. Somehow, it was thought that the big bird so liked by everyone arrived in England by the same route--and therefore this bird was given the name "Turkey".

About 1561 the country raising of turkeys had become so popular that even the farmers often had turkey for Christmas dinner; early accounts record a Christmas fare as:

> "Meat, mutton and pork--dressed pies of the best.
> Pig, veal, goose and capon--and turkey well drest"

It was not surprising, therefore, that the early pilgrims brought turkeys with them when they came to settle America. One can appreciate, however, their surprise to find the turkey already one of the most plentiful foods of the American Indians.

William Woods of the Massachusetts colony wrote about 1630 that

> "The Turky is a very large Bird, of a blacke colour, yet
> white in flesh; much bigger than our English Turky. He
> hath the use of his long legs so ready that he can runne
> as fast as a Dogge, and flye as well as a Goose: of these
> sometimes there will be forty, three-score and a hundred of
> of a flocke, sometimes more and sometimes lesse; their
> feeding is Acornes, Hawes, and Berries, some of them haunt
> to frequent our English corne: In winter when the snow

covers the ground, they resort to the Sea shore to look for Shrimps, & such smal Fishes at low tides......"

Although the wild turkey was a plentiful food for the early settlers, it was almost exterminated by hunters by the year 1850. Fortunately, some survived in several of the southern states and in the Nittany mountains of Pennsylvania. It remains today in fairly good numbers and ranks with the black bear as one of the most highly prized sporting trophies to be taken in Pennsylvania.

The early settlers usually kept a few turkeys in their barnyards which often had to forage quite far for food. Some wandered off with wild flocks. Oftentimes, a wild turkey tom would fly in and mate with some of the domestic hens. This crossing acted to improve the viability of the domestic stock and also the size of the domestic turkeys. Some of the first deliberate crosses were made in the area of Narragansett Bay, Rhode Island (about 1830-1840). A few years later farmers in the vicinity of Point Judith, Rhode Island performed still another cross of the Narragansett turkey with the wild turkey and named the new variety the "Bronze" turkey. The original white turkeys probably were genetic mutations or "sports" of the bronze turkey.

MANAGEMENT AND NUTRITION OF THE MODERN TURKEY

Much of the research in poultry nutrition has been conducted with chickens. This research, and its application to practical broiler and laying hen nutrition, has been the subject of a book by Scott, Nesheim and Young (1982). While much of the basic nutritional information in that book can be applied to other species, such as the turkey, many important differences exist between chicken and turkey nutrition. Lacking good information on the specifics of turkey nutrition, many turkey growers and feed manufacturers have used the information concerning chickens directly, often with less than optimal results.

It appeared desirable, therefore, to review the special nutritional requirements of starting, growing, and finishing turkeys as well as those of turkey breeders and to submit this review as a supplement to the above referenced book "NUTRITION OF THE CHICKEN" by Scott, Nesheim and Young. It is the purpose of this book to serve as such a supplement.

No effort will be made here to cover the basic aspects of such nutrition-related matters as the metabolism and biochemical utilization of energy, protein, vitamin and essential inorganic elements. These subjects are amply covered in the reference work--"NUTRITION OF THE CHICKEN" (1982). In most instances, all of these nutrients are metabolized similarly in chickens and turkeys. Special emphasis will be placed, where applicable, on all metabolic mechanisms that are known to differ between chickens and turkeys. An example of this is the special high requirement of turkeys for niacin because of the inately high level of picolinic acid carboxylase in the livers of turkeys compared to that in chickens. This enzyme prevents the turkey from obtaining an appreciable amount of niacin from the metabolism of the amino acid, tryptophan. Other differences, such as those that exist in the symptoms of folic acid deficiency in these species also will be fully described and discussed in terms of their importance in practical turkey production.

The anatomy and physiology of the turkey differ markedly from the characteristics of chickens. Some of these differences must be considered in the proper nutrition of the turkey during its many stages of development and/or reproduction. Because of the heavy and broad-breasted characteristics of the turkey, this species is particularly subject to leg weaknesses. There is evidence that the gastic juices of the turkey are not as acid as those of the chicken and thus the turkey utilizes anhydrous dicalcium phosphate poorly because it does not dissolve in the proventriculus sufficiently well for absorption in the duodenum of the young poult.

Studies on the nutrient composition of turkey meat, conducted by the author (Scott, 1956, 1958, 1959) show that the edible portion of turkey is higher in protein and essential amino acids than any other meat and very low in calories and cholesterol.

Following these studies, the National Turkey Federation and the Poultry and Egg National Board conducted a nationwide education and advertising campaign. Using highway billboards, advertisements in magazines and lectures to dieticians, food and nutrition reporters and others, the excellent nutritional qualities of turkey meat were portrayed to the consumers (Figure 1.1).

Studies by others (USDA, 1979) have also shown the high nutritive values of turkey meat. Earlier studies on this subject had been conducted by Harshaw et al. (1943), but these studies were undertaken using the turkeys of poor body conformation such as those shown as the early breeds in Figure 1.2.

In 1959, Yang, Clark and Vail of Purdue University conducted an experiment with rats to determine the biological value of turkey meat compared to that of casein. Turkey leg meat was freeze-dried and added at graded levels to provide 5, 10, 15, and 20% protein in a basic diet that was adequate in all nutrients except for protein and amino acids. Similarly, casein was added to provide equivalent levels of protein. At the critical protein levels of 5 and 10%, the dried turkey meat promoted better weight gains, better efficiency of food utilization and better efficiency of protein utilization than were obtained with equivalent levels of casein.

Figure 1.1 Early advertising by the National Turkey Federation and the Poultry and Egg National Board demonstrating the high nutritional values of turkey meat at economical prices.

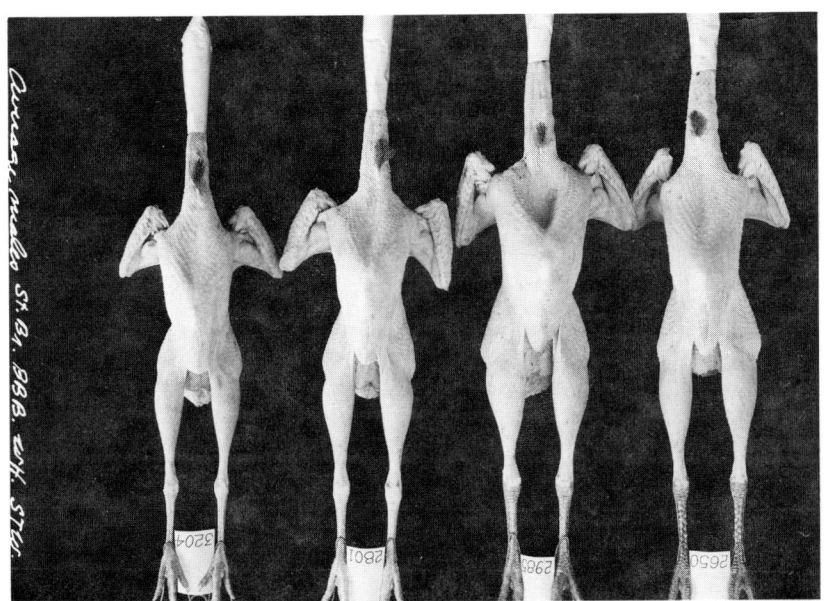

Figure 1.2   The marked genetic improvements in body conformation of market turkeys. Top photo shows "New York Dressed" carcasses in the year 1941. From left to right are shown representatives of Standard White, White Holland, "Broad Breasted" Bronze and Standard Bronze breeds of that time. Lower photo shows representatives of <u>present-day</u>, <u>oven-ready</u> carcasses of hen and tom turkeys.

Because the turkey poult contains a low amount of carcass energy and a very high level of protein in the tissues being produced during growth, the protein requirement of starting and young growing poults is higher than the requirements of chickens and other species of poultry. Thus, the energy:protein ratio of the diet of young poults is considerably narrower than that of young broiler chickens. Due to the long growth period of the turkey, from hatching to near maturity, compared with the short growth period of broilers, the requirements for protein, and energy and the level of fat in the diet is much more important for turkeys than for growing and finishing broilers.

The nutrient content of market turkey flesh and skin, compared with that of market broilers or fryers, is shown in Table 1.1. This shows the higher protein content of turkeys versus chickens. The results of studies by the United States Department of Agriculture (USDA, 1979), presented, in part, in Table 1.1, show that turkey meat also contains higher levels of potassium, zinc, riboflavin, folic acid, vitamin B_6, vitamin B_{12}, methionine and lysine per 100 grams of edible meat than are present in an equal amount of chicken meat. The higher niacin level in chickens already has been explained in terms of the greater synthesis of niacin from tryptophan in chickens than in turkeys. The higher linoleic acid of chickens naturally accompanies the higher fat content. Both chickens and turkeys contain a healthful mix of polyunsaturated and monounsaturated fatty acids.

Thus, the turkey has been shown to be a concentrated source of desirable nutrients.

It is understandable, therefore, that the nutritional requirements of the turkey are higher than those of chickens and of most other species.

This work has focused attention on turkey as an economical, healthful food. It has caused the general public to accept turkey as a good everyday food rather than simply a gourmet food for special occasions.

The demand for turkey increased in restaraunts and in the general household, bringing about a need for increased turkey production and thus an increase in the turkey industry.

Evolution of Knowledge Concerning the Genetics, Disease Control, Management, and Nutrition of Market Turkeys

Although a considerable knowledge existed prior to World War II concerning the origin and characteristics of the then-known breeds of turkeys, no appreciable turkey-producing industry occurred until the 1940's when, due to the war, red meat became scarce in the United States. Prior to World War II turkeys were produced in small numbers on family farms and the only important

Table 1.1. Comparison of the Nutrient Composition of Flesh and Skin of Market Chickens and Turkeys.

Nutrients	Chicken (Amounts/100 gm)	Turkey (Amounts/100 gm)
Protein, gm	18.6	20.4
Food energy, Kcal.	215	160
Fat, gm	15.0	8.0
Calcium, mg	11	15
Phosphorus, mg	147	178
Sodium, mg	70	65
Potassium, mg	189	266
Zinc, mg	1.3	2.2
Vitamin B_1, mcg	60	64
" B_2, mcg	120	155
" B_6, mcg	310	400
" B_{12}, mcg	0.31	0.4
Niacin, mcg	6800	4100
Pantothenic acid, mcg	910	810
Folic acid, mcg	6.0	8.0
Methionine, gm	0.493	0.574
Lysine, gm	1.51	1.86
Linoleic acid, gm	2.88	1.70

sale of turkeys occurred at Thanksgiving. Approximately thirty million turkeys were sufficient to take care of the annual needs of this country prior to 1940, and most of these were consumed at the Thanksgiving dinner. By the end of the war, turkey production in the USA had doubled to approximately sixty million. Since the population of the country had not increased, this meant that the per capita consumption of turkey had doubled in about five years. The results of a survey conducted by the American Feed Manufacturers Association in 1952 showed that annual per capita consumption of turkey meat had quadrupled over the previous 15 years. More than 200 million turkeys were produced in 1986. This increased demand for turkey meat caused turkey production to become a very profitable industry. As with any successful business, those involved began to look for means of improving the quality of the product and the efficiency of production.

Genetic Improvements

Marsden amd Martin in their book (TURKEY MANAGEMENT, 1939), refer to the book entitled AMERICAN STANDARD OF PERFECTION, which indicated that turkeys were considered to be a single CLASS of poultry, and that within that class there existed only one BREED which was divided into six VARIETIES. However, it was noted that in popular usage, these varieties were referred to as "BREEDS". This terminology will be used here in order to avoid confusion in the field.

Thus, the "BREEDS" that were recognized in 1939 were the BRONZE, the NARRAGANSETT, the WHITE HOLLAND, the BOURBON RED, the BLACK, and the SLATE. All were derived from the North American wild turkey, <u>Meleagris gallopavo</u>, which consisted of several varieties and ranged, originally, from New England to central Mexico.

Many geneticists and turkey breeders were responsible for the development of the breeds and strains that exist today. Some made tremendous improvements by genetic selection within a breed, particularly within the Bronze breed, which had the broadest breast and best growth rates of the various breeds. Other improvements were made by crossing some of the breeds. It is of interest that the terminology at that time was such that, in order to qualify as "broad-breasted", the turkey breast must be found to measure at least four inches in width. Contrasting this with the very broad breasts of present-day turkeys, often measuring more than eight inches in width (Figure 1.1), it is apparent that tremendous genetic improvements were achieved.
At Cornell University, the EMPIRE WHITE turkey represented the first development of a truly Broad-Breasted White turkey. This was accomplished by crossing the White Holland breed with a newly-developed truly Broad-Breasted Bronze breed. The first generation of this cross were all bronze in color. However, upon crossing the siblings with each other, the resulting poults existed as 50% bronze and 50% white. Crossing these whites with

the original Broad-Breasted Bronze produced siblings which again were all bronze in color. Crossing these with each other gave offspring of which 75% were bronze and 25% were white. These whites were crossed back with the Broad-Breasted Bronze, and when these siblings were crossed with each other there were 7 bronze poults for each white poult produced--but these Empire White turkeys were almost as Broad-Breasted as the original Broad-Breasted Bronze and when the white turkeys were bred to each other they produced only Broad-Breasted White poults. Many, if not all, of our present-day Broad-Breasted White turkey strains were evolved in a similar manner followed by further genetic selection for desirable traits.

Other developments of note were the Beltsville Small White breed, evolved by Marsden of the USDA; and some very large and fast-growing strains of both Broad-Breasted Bronze and White breeds developed by several turkey breeders in California and elsewhere.

Some of the objectives accomplished in these breeding programs were as follows:

1) Rapid economical growth with high dressing percentage;
2) Relatively high egg production over an extended period of time; good fertility and hatchability;
3) Hens ideal size for family use; toms excellent for restaurants, institutions and for further processing;
4) White feathers which have commercial value; white pin feathers inconspicuous on the dressed carcass;
5) Early maturity with acceptable body finish;
6) Reduced tendency toward leg weaknesses and improved resistance to development of breast blisters.

By 1960, commercial production of large, meaty, fast-growing turkeys was being accomplished in all of the states of the United States and in several other countries. In 1961, the author participated in the 10th Annual Meeting of the British Turkey Growers Association held in Harrogate, England and attended by nearly 100 turkey producers, some of whom produced in excess of 50,000 turkeys per year.

Studies also were undertaken to improve the genetics of reproduction in breeding turkeys. Nestor (1971), selecting for increased egg production over seven generations, produced an increase of 18 eggs per hen during the first 84 days, and 37 eggs per hen over the first 180 day period. This selection for high egg production caused an initial loss in body weights at 16 and 24 weeks of age, but this loss was recovered by two generations of selecting for increased 16-week body weights and at the same time the high rate of egg production was maintained. These methods have helped to improve egg production in today's turkeys.

Progress in Disease Control

Prior to 1940, when most turkeys ran in the barnyard with the chickens, mortality in the turkeys was very high, particularly from the disease known as blackhead. Although this disease had been recognized and studied for many years, it was not eradicated from commercial flocks until after Dr. E. N Moore of the Cornell Veterinary College described the cause and symptoms of the disease and presented management methods required to control it. At the same time, Dr. W. A. Billings, of the University of Minnesota took on the project of preaching the necessity of stringent sanitation and of keeping turkeys strictly separated not only from their own droppings, but also from the droppings of chickens which had been shown to be carriers of the blackhead organism, _Histomonas meleagridis_, even though the chickens do not contract the disease. This advice was adopted by most, if not all successful turkey producers, and the resulting improved management practices were largely responsible for the development of profitable turkey production and, thus a turkey industry.

Turkeys were subject to many other diseases--so many that some people wondered if turkey production would ever be profitable. However, veterinary research now has brought about development of vaccines and has worked out management methods that sucessfully control most diseases.

Improved Management Practices

In the early 1900's it was thought that turkeys must be given free range--the more lush the pasture, the better. Usually, the turkeys ranged with the chickens and perhaps some ducks and a few geese. Jull, in 1929, conducted a survey of suggestions concerning the type of research needed to help make turkey production a more efficient and profitable enterprise. Several bulletins were prepared (Alder, 1946; Misner, 1946; Smith, 1947; Marsden, 1952) to advise turkey growers regarding the latest methods of turkey production to that time.

After the need to control blackhead by improved management was recognized, many innovative rearing methods were initiated. One of these was the confinement rearing of turkeys on slat floors. The "greens" thought to be essential were cut and brought daily. This kept the turkeys away from chickens, and from most of their own droppings, and largely prevented blackhead, but also brought out certain other difficulties, especially an increase in the incidence and severity of leg weaknesses and breast blisters.
With the development of improved feeds, which will be described later, it was soon realized that turkeys did not need pasture or "greens". Most turkeys today, therefore, are reared in dry lots.

Provision of shelters from rain and wind and the placement of the feeders came under study. It was found that the shelters should not be near the feeders and water, such that the turkeys would tend to congregate in one place and cause a build-up of droppings and thus an increased "disease level" especially during wet weather.

In a hilly or inclined range, it is desirable to initially place the feeders and waterers at the bottom of the hill and gradually move them up the hill so that disease-carrying manure does not wash down upon the turkeys during heavy rains.

The design of the feeders was found to be important. Feeders should not have a high front board or any structure upon which the turkeys can lean and thus develop breast blisters.

For turkeys reared in confinement it is now possible to better control environmental temperature by using good insulation and fans for proper air circulation. Carver (1987) of the British ADAS Gleadthorpe Experimental Husbandry Farm reported that tom turkeys reared to 24 weeks of age grow best at a house temperature of 18 degrees C. (65 degrees F.). However, this temperature may not give the best feed conversions. It is well recognized that turkeys can grow quite well within the range of temperatures up to that which exceeds their "upper critical temperature" (About 33 degrees C--91 degrees F).

Adoption of artificial insemination

As the size of the turkey toms was increased, mating became more difficult and often caused severe harm to the hens even when they were equipped with saddles.

In order to be assured of 90+% fertility, turkey breeders initiated the practice of artificial insemination which is now universally practiced.

Research has been accomplished to create best methods for handling the semem (Bagpai and Brown,1964; Graham, et al.,1982; Cecil, 1984; McIntyre, and associates, 1985,1986; Bakst, 1985), and for carrying out the ensemination process. Ingenious passageways have been constructed through which the female turkeys pass, one by one, while the inseminator sits in a "dugout" beside the passageway in such a position that the hens are exactly at eye level. This permits rapid insemination of large numbers of hens with a minimum of strain on the person doing the artificial inseminating.

Length of daylight was studied by Moultrie et al. (1955), who found that turkeys exposed to 10 or 24 hours of day length showed quite different molting characteristics. Turkeys reared at 10 hours day lengths did not molt any post-juvenile wing feathers and very few post-juvenile tail feathers. Those reared with 24 hour daylengths, molted many post-juvenile wing feathers at 17 weeks of age, and molted significantly more of their post-juvenile tail feathers. The variations in daylength did not effect the time required for the individual feathers to grow to maturity, indicating that rearing at 10 hours of daylength produces good feathering with less loss due to molting.

This research, together with that of many others, has been responsible for our ability, today, to produce turkey eggs and poults the year around, which was not possible when stimulation of the breeding turkeys was dependent only on changes in natural daylengths.

Rearing the poults

Starve-outs, according to Pomeroy (1975), accounted for 29% of the total turkey poult mortality in Minnesota in 1971. Indeed, total management losses were 62% against only 38% due to pathological diseases.

Difficulty in inducing baby poults to eat and drink has been recognized by turkey farmers throughout history. Many different procedures have been used in the past to induce them to eat and drink:
1) Bright colored marbles are placed in the waterers to attract the attention of the poults;
2) A light of at least 40 Watts is placed directly above the feeders and waterers;
3) Feeders and waterers are placed initially so that they are at the very edge of the hover, approximately 1/2 inside and 1/2 outside the hover, under the light.

All of these practices are helpful, but sometimes do not appear to be sufficient to prevent starve-outs.

Smith and Phillips (1959) found that green lights, placed directly above the feeders and waterers were very helpful in getting baby poults off to a good start. Feed consumption for the four colors of lights tested were: 42.2% for green, 20.2% for yellow, 19.5% for orange and 18% for red. Cooper (1971) showed that green-colored feed was consumed in largest quantities when turkey poults were given a choice of seven different colored feeds. This finding is not used commercially to the extent that it should be.

Energy content of the starting diet is very important for the prevention of starve-outs. Baby poults apparently fail to recognize high-fiber, low-energy diets as food. They may peck at it a few times and walk away even though hungry. High-energy feeds, especially those dressed with 2-3% fat, are consumed much more readily.

Chilson and Patrick (1946) demonstrated the importance of supplying baby poults with feed and water as soon as possible after hatching. When feed and water were withheld for 24, 48, or 72 hours after hatching, the resultant mortality was 4.8%, 11.5%, and 29.3% respectively, up to 12 weeks of age.

Rearing breeders

Helene Cecil (1984) found that light restriction (6 hours light and 18 hours darkness) during the prebreeding period, had no effect upon the body weights or semen production at 35 weeks of age. Siopes (1983), however, reported that intermittent lighting (i.e. 2 hrs light, 11 hrs dark, 2 hrs light, 9 hrs dark) maintained body weight, semen quantity and quality equal to that of the controls receiving 15 hrs light and 9 hrs dark. A saving of 73% on the electricity needed for lighting was found with the intermittent lighting regime versus the control program. The intermittent lighting program was found to be especially efficient in hot weather of summer.

Hetzel (1940) reported excellent fertility in toms that were given increased daylengths five weeks before the hens were placed under increased daylengths. To obtain maximum fertility in the first eggs laid, hens should be mated or inseminated with viable semen within three weeks prior to the onset of egg production. Sexten and McCartney (1973) found that increasing the daylength of turkey hens at 32 to 36 weeks of age gave best over-all reproductive performance.

Mitchell et al. (1962), Anderson, et al. (1963), and Voitle et al. (1973) reported that feed restriction, especially during the 12 to 24 week growth period, is effective in bringing turkey hens to sexual maturity at a specified weight and age.

Balloun (1973) and Moore et al. (1983) reported that feed restriction of toms during the prebreeding period either has no effect or causes a slight improvement in subsequent reproductive capacity.

In summary, light restriction must be practiced to obtain hatching eggs at all times of the year. Feed restriction should be practiced only when necessary to achieve desired body weights.

Evolution of Our Knowledge of Turkey Nutrition

In 1958, W. W. Cravens and the author presented a brief outline history of " Fifty Years of Progress in Turkey Nutrition" at the Golden Convention of the American Feed Manufacturers Association held in Chicago.

The discussion began with conditions in 1908 when the pamphlets on feeding baby poults recommended "common sting nettle chopped

Figure 1.3 Dr. W. W. Cravens (right) discussing with the author the progress in turkey nutrition made during the 50 years prior to 1958.
(American Feed Manufacturers Association Golden Convention, 1958)

with hard-boiled egg and a little shake of red pepper". As the turkeys grew "a little stale bread soaked in sweet or clabbered milk and squeezed dry" was mixed with the egg and nettle. In the morning the turkeys also received a "good feeding of lettuce and a little chopped onion". They also got "a little tincture of iron three times a week". After the turkeys were old enough to go out on range they were supposed to forage for most of their food. Grasshoppers, other insects and such foods as wild strawberries were mentioned as good foods along with grasses and legumes. Small amounts of "scratch grains" were fed when necessary.

By 1945, much had been learned concerning the needs for protein, amino acids, vitamins and minerals but little was known about the quantitative requirements of turkeys for these nutrients. Some fairly good turkey rations had been worked out by trial and error but they were very expensive and too high in fiber and low in energy for the promotion of maximum growth and certainly were not suitable for best efficiency or economy of feed utilization.

The 1958 turkey rations discussed by Cravens and Scott were scientifically formulated using the nutritional information available at that time (Figure 1.3), but it was agreed that "many improvements were still needed in turkey rearing and feeding".

During the 30 years since that Chicago meeting many important improvements have been made. The example turkey rations presented in Chapter 2 (Tables 2.6-2.17 and 2.21-2.32) incorporate these findings which now produce diets capable of promoting growth and economy of feed utilization up to the maximum genetic potentials of the turkeys.

Marsden and Martin, in 1939, extolled the great contribution of the turkey as one of the best converters of grains and byproducts into high quality meat. They indicated that "The average turkey when finished for market at 28 weeks of age has only consumed from four to four and three-quarters pounds of feed for each pound of live body weight, assuming some range is available. If confined, the ratio is about five and one-half to one. The average chicken broiler at 10 to 12 weeks weighing two pounds has consumed about four pounds of feed for each pound of body weight. However, a three to three and one-half pound fryer has consumed at least five pounds of feed for each pound of gain and an 8-pound capon between seven and eight pounds of feed for each pound of live body weight".

Contrast these data with today's growth rates and efficiencies of feed utilization. Broilers now average about four to four and one-half pounds live weight at seven weeks of age and achieve these weights on about 1.9 to 2.0 pounds of feed per pound of live body weight. Turkey hens are marketed at about 16-18 weeks of age weighing about 14-18 pounds and with an efficiency of feed utilization of about 2.8 to 3.0; toms, marketed at 19-24 weeks of age weigh 25-35 pounds and also have an efficiency of feed utilization of about 2.5-3.0. This is accomplished with rations that are lower in cost than the 1939 rations would be today because of the high levels of milk products, alfalfa meal and other expensive ingredients that they contained. These ingredients are not now required because of our superior knowledge of nutritional requirements and of the nutrient contents of all common poultry feedstuffs, thus allowing us to formulate feeds on a scientific, least-cost basis.

The history of the development of our present knowledge concerning the nutrition of the turkey may be of interest. At the time referred to by Marsden and Martin above (1939), little scientific research had been conducted on the nutritional requirements of turkeys. It was popularly believed by most turkey producers that turkeys could make good use of fiber and indeed that turkeys required a diet that was fairly high in fiber. If the turkeys were being reared on range where they could get plenty of fibrous forage, no effort was made to add fibrous ingredients to the concentrate mixture being fed. However, diets for turkeys being reared in confinement contained high amounts of bran, alfalfa meal oats, etc. and were, therefore, very low in metabolizable energy. Protein, fat and fiber contents of some typical commercial turkey starting rations of the mid-1940's are shown in Table 1.2. Though low in energy, these diets contained generous amounts of dried whey. liver and glandular meal, dried brewers' yeast and fish meal and thus would be very expensive today.

One of the first nutritional studies of higher-energy diets for turkey poults was conducted by Scott, Heuser and Norris in 1948. The results of these studies showed that starting poults required a higher energy diet than that being used at that time, and that a higher protein level was needed with the higher energy level. The studies showed a need in the starting diet for at least 1200 Kcal. metabolizable energy per pound of diet, and that approximately 28% protein was needed with this level of energy. Indeed, further experiments showed improved growth and efficiency of feed utilization with starting energy levels of up to 1400 Kcal/lb and corresponding protein levels up to 32%. The levels of energy and protein chosen for these diets depended upon the magnitude of the improvement in growth and efficiency versus the increased cost of the higher energy, higher protein diets, a practice still followed today.

Recommendation of these levels of energy and protein created a furor among turkey breeders and turkey growers. Letters were written by the breeders warning growers against using these "wild" recommendations. It was indicated that protein levels above 24% would "burn up" the poults--and the breeders certainly would not "guarantee" livability of their poults if these high

Table 1.2. Protein, fat, and fiber contents of commercial turkey starter rations of the mid-1940's and mean 4-week weights of poults fed these rations.

Ration	Protein	Fat	Fiber	Mean poult wts, 4 wks.
	%	%	%	gms
A	24.7	5.3	7.3	419
B	24.0	4.5	7.2	368
C	24.0	3.8	7.2	312

Scott, Heuser and Norris, 1948

energy-high protein recommendations were followed.

In time, however, a better understanding of the nutritional principle known as the energy:protein ratio was acheived and all commercial turkey rations were formulated on this basis. This, together with many other basic findings in turkey nutrition have led to the dramatic improvement in growth and efficiency of feed utilization which has been responsible for the efficient, economical production of turkeys as one of our most highly nutritious foods.

Although improvements in genetics, disease control and management all have played important roles in the development of our present, highly efficient turkey industry, these developments would serve for naught without the knowledge achieved in turkey nutrition.

Feeding the breeders

The effect of varying the environmental temperature, and of using high dietary fat levels, on reproductive performance of Large White turkey breeding hens was studied by Rosebrough and Steele (1985). Varying the 24-hour temperature from 12 to 27 degrees C (giving an average temperature for the 24 hours of 21 degrees C), resulted in improved egg production, improved hatchability of fertile eggs and improved efficiency of feed utilization for egg production, as well as a decrease in broodiness in the hens compared to those maintained at a constant temperature of 21 degrees C at all times of the day.

The hens fed the high-fat diet (17% protein; fat level at 47% of total calories) were much more efficient and, under the conditions of vaying temperature, produced more eggs, and better hatchability of eggs than those fed a low-fat diet (17% protein; fat at 8% of total calories). The high-fat diet produced a lower liver lipid and lower <u>in vitro</u> lipogenesis, probably by providing a preformed fatty acid pool for egg lipids.

It is the purpose of this book to present the present status of turkey nutrition and to discuss feeds and feeding of turkeys.

REFERENCES

Alder, B. 1946. Economical turkey production in Utah. Economical feed important factor in profits. Farm & Home Science 7:1 Utah Agricultural Experiment Station.

Anderson, D. L., J. R. Smyth, Jr., and R. E. Gleason 1963. Effect of restricted feeding during the growing period on reproductive performance of Large White type turkeys. Poultry Sci. 42: 8-15.

Bajpai, P. K. and K. I. Brown 1964. Effects of potassium and magnesium chlorides on the metabolic activity and fertility of turkey spermatozoa. Poultry Sci. 43: 459-461.

Bakst, M. R. 1985. Zinc reduces turkey sperm oxygen uptake in vitro. Poultry Sci. 64: 564-566.

Barrett, F.N., C. G. Card, and A. Berridge 1946. Feeding and confinement rearing of turkeys during 1944. Michigan Agricultural Experiment Station Quarterly Bull. 29 (2): 88-101, Lake City, MI.

Carver, R. 1987. The right temperature for good turkey performance. Misset International Poultry 3 (3): 22-23.

Cecil, Helene C. 1984. Effect of dietary protein and light restriction on body weight and semen production of breeder male turkeys. Poultry Sci. 63:1175-1183.

Chilson, W. T., and H. Patrick 1946. Effect of withholding feed and water on early poult mortality and growth. Poultry Sci. 25: 86-87.

Cooper, J. B. 1971. Colored feeds for turkey poults. Poultry Sci. 50: 1892-1893.

Feeding Forum 1952. Turkey production...based upon exciting procedures. American Feed Manufacturers Assoc., Chicago.

Forbush, E. H., and J. B. May 1955. A NATURAL HISTORY OF AMERICAN BIRDS OF EASTERN AND CENTRAL NORTH AMERICA. Bramhall House.

Gerstell, R., and W. H. Long 1939. Biological variations in wild turkeys and the significance of management. Research Bul. No. 2, 60 pp. Pa. Game Comm., Harrisburg, Pa.

Graham, E. F., D. S. Nelson and M. K. L. Schmehl 1982. Development of extender and techniques for frozen turkey semen. I. Development; II. Fertility trials. Poultry Sci. 61: 550-563.

Harshaw, H. M., W.L. Kellogg, R.R. Rector and S.J Marsden 1943. The composition of turkeys of different varieties and strains. Poultry Sci. 22:126

Hetzel, R. D. 1940. Turkeys fertile under lights. Pa. State Agric. Exp. Sta. Bull. 399: 53-55.

Jull, M. A. 1929. Research work on turkey raising. Poultry Sci. 8:129-132.

Marsden, S. J. 1952. Turkey raising. Farmers' Bull. No. 1409, USDA.

Marsden, S. J., and J. H. Martin 1939. TURKEY MANAGEMENT, The Interstate, Danville, IL.

McCartney, M.G., J.W. Wyne and V.D. Chamberlin 1956. Turkeys grow as well in confinement as on range. OHIO FARM AND HOME RESEARCH.

McIntyre, D. R. and V. L. Christensen 1985. Effect of initial insemination and insemination interval on fertility in turkey hens. Poultry Sci. 64:1549-1552.

McIntyre, D. R., V. L. Christensen and L. G. Bagley 1986. Effect of sperm numbers per insemination following early or late initial insemination in turkeys. Poultry Sci. 65:1400-1404.

Milby, T.T., and R. Penquite 1940. Feeding grasshoppers to turkeys. Poultry Sci. 19: 332-336.

Misner, E. G. 1946. Costs and returns for the turkey enterprise. Bull. No. 827, Cornell University Agricultural Experiment Station, Ithaca, N

Moore, E. N. 1950. Blackhead (Histomoniasis) can be controlled. Cornell Extension Bull. 806, New York State College of Agriculture, Ithaca, NY.

Moultrie, F., C. D. Mueller and L. F. Payne. 1955. Molting and growth of individual feathers in turkeys exposed to 10 or 24 hours of daily light. Poultry Sci. 34: 383-388.

Nestor, K. E. 1971. Genetics of growth and reproduction in the turkey. 3. Further selection for increased egg production. Poultry Sci. 50: 1672-1682.

Payne, L.F. 1959. Turkeys grown in confinement and on range. Poultry Sci. 38:1087-1094.

Pomeroy, B. S. 1975. Death losses by cause. Feedstuffs.

Rosebrough, R. W., and N. C. Steele 1985. Effect of dietary fat and environment on lipogenesis by Large White breeder turkeys. Poultry Sci. 64: 1170-1176.

Scott, M. L. 1956. Composition of turkey meat. J. Amer. Diet. Assoc. 32: 941-944.

Scott, M. L. 1958. Composition of turkey meat. II. Cholesterol content and fatty acid composition. J. Amer. Diet. Assoc. 34: 154-156.

Scott, M. L. 1959. Composition of turkey meat. III. Essential amino acid composition. J. Amer. Diet. Assoc. 35: 247-249.

Scott, M. L. 1957. The nutrient composition of turkey meat. In TURKEY --HIGHEST IN PROTEIN--LOW IN FAT. The National Turkey Federation, Mount Morris, IL, and Poultry & Egg National Board, St.Charles, IL.

Scott, M. L., G. F. Heuser and L. C. Norris 1948. Studies in turkey nutrition using a purified diet. Poultry Sci. 27: 770-772.

Scott, M. L., G. F. Heuser and L. C. Norris. 1948. Energy, protein and unidentified vitamins in poult nutrition. Poultry Sci. 27: 773-780.

Scott, M. L., M. C. Nesheim, and R. J. Young 1982. NUTRITION OF THE CHICKEN, 3rd ED., M. L. Scott & Assoc. P. O. Box 816, Ithaca, NY 14850.

Sexten, W. E., and M. G. McCartney 1973. The effect of age at lighting on reproduction in the turkey hen. Poultry Sci. 52:

516-520.
Siopes, T. D. 1983. Effect of intermittent lighting on energy saving and semen characteristics of breeder tom turkeys. Poultry Sci. 62: 2265-2270.
Smith, E. Y. 1947. Growing turkeys. Cornell Extension Bull. 717. N. Y. State College of Agr., Ithaca, NY.
Smith, L. T., and R. E. Phillips 1959. Influence of colored neon lights on feed consumption in poults. Poultry Sci. 38: 1248.
USDA 1979. Composition of foods. Agricultural Handbook 8-5, Poultry Products. U.S. Govt. Printing Off.,Washington, D.C.
Van Tienhoven, A. 1958. Diluents for turkey semen. Poultry Sci. 37: 47-53.
Yang, S. P., H. E. Clark., and G. E. Vail. 1959. Nutritional value of turkey proteins. Utilization of turkey proteins as compared with casein, using the young rat as the experimental animal. J. Amer. Diet. Assoc. 35: 1251-1.

CHAPTER 2

ENERGY, PROTEIN AND AMINO ACID REQUIREMENTS OF TURKEYS

As indicated in Chapter 1, early turkey growers and breeders thought that the turkey could utilize fibrous feedstuffs and thus fed very low-energy rations. They realized that the turkey required more protein at the start than did starting chicks. Experience had shown that a level of 24% protein was needed in these low-energy diets.

During the late 1940's and early 1950's most nutritionists understood the important relationship between the energy and the protein of the diet. Combs and associates of the University of Maryland published papers describing the importance of the Calorie:Protein (C/P) Ratio (Donaldson, Combs and Romoser, 1956).

At Cornell, the author together with Heuser and Norris (1948) initiated studies with turkey poults, using a high-energy, purified diet which promoted much better growth and much improved efficiency of feed utilization, compared with that obtained with the commercial turkey starter diet used as a control ration.

This finding led these workers to investigate the cause of the superiority of the purified diet. Experiments were conducted comparing the results with the three most popular commercial starting rations being used in New York State in the mid-1940's. Proximate composition and results with these rations were given in Table 1.2. The best growth, obtained with commercial Ration A, resulted in an average poult weight of 419 grams at four weeks of age. Ration C supported a 4-week weight of only 312 grams. These were very poor growth rates compared with the weight of 545 grams obtained in the poults receiving the purified diet, and the average weight of 576 grams obtained when the purified diet was supplemented with 2% yeast plus 2% liver concentrate.

The purified diet used in these studies contained 35% protein and was composed of casein, gelatin, corn starch, soybean oil plus vitamins and minerals and 3.5% cellophane as a source of fiber. The calculated metabolizable energy content of the diet was 3750 Kcal per kilogram or about 1700 Kcal/lb. It was hypothesized that the superior results with this diet were due either to its high energy or high protein or both. A low-energy, high-fiber practical diet (Diet D) was formulated to simulate the composition of the commercial turkey starting rations. This ration contained 10% wheat bran, 16% standard wheat middlings, 10% oats, 10% alfalfa meal, plus some corn, soybean meal, fish meal, meat and bone meal, yeast, liver meal, and dried whey. It was supplemented with vitamins and minerals up to the levels used in the purified diet. The calculated energy content of this diet was 1074 Kcal metabolizable energy per pound; the protein was 24.17%. When this diet was fed alone or supplemented with soybean meal or casein to bring the protein up to 30 or 36%, or with 10% additional liver meal, the growth on the basic diet was similar to that obtained with the commercial rations and no appreciable improvements were obtained with any of the supplements.

Consequently, a practical-type, high energy basal ration (Diet E) was formulated using more corn meal plus flour middlings and rolled oats in place of the fibrous ingredients (bran, middlings, ground whole oats, and alfalfa meal) used in the low-energy ration. Calculations indicated that this diet contained about 1200 Kcal metabolizable energy per pound and about 30% protein.

When the low-energy diet was compared to the purified diet, the weights of the poults receiving diet D at four weeks of age averaged only 434 grams, versus 586 grams with the purified diet. Increasing the protein in diet D did not cause any significant increase in growth of the poults.

However, when the higher-energy Diet E was fed, in three separate experiments, the growth of the poults at four weeks of age was similar, in each instance, to that of poults receiving the purified diet and showed an increase in growth of up to 50% greater than that obtained with Diet D or with any of the three commercial turkey starter rations used.

Subsequent studies at Cornell University and elsewhere demonstrated the importance of using diets of adequate energy content and showed the range of energy levels within which poults can readily obtain sufficient energy for maximum growth--and the levels of protein needed with each energy level and at each stage of growth (Atkinson, et al., 1957; Day and Hill, 1957; Donaldson, et al., 1958; Dunkelgod and Thayer, 1957; Balloun, et al., 1959; Hurwitz, et al., 1983; Sell, et al., 1985; Summers, et al., 1985). This range of energy levels and the corresponding protein requirements are given in Table 2.1.

Energy values for turkeys

Slinger, Sibbald and Pepper (1964), in studies of the relative abilities of two breeds of chickens and two varieties of turkeys to metabolize dietary energy, found that the chickens and the turkeys utilized the high-energy diets equally well, but that the turkeys were able to obtain slightly more energy than the chickens from the high-fiber feedstuffs. These findings were confirmed by Leeson, et al.(1974) who found that whereas corn had an equal ME value for both chicks and poults, the value for oats was 8% greater for the poults than for chicks.

Nevertheless, the few studies that have been conducted on the metabolizable energy (ME) content of feedstuffs for turkeys indicate that, for the most part, the ME values determined for chickens as given by Scott, Nesheim and Young (1982) are sufficiently applicable that they can be used, and are being used routinely, in the formulation of practical feeds for turkeys. Examination of cecal microflora of turkeys (Bedbury and Duke, 1983) indicated that the feeding of high-fiber diets caused the development of increased numbers of cellulolytic microorganisms. However, this breakdown of cellulose occurs too far down the intestinal tract to be of much value to the host turkey.

Amino acid requirements of growing turkeys

Amino acid requirements of turkeys were studied by Bird, Kratzer, et al., Balloun et al., Sherman, et al., Snetsinger, et al., Potter et al., Hurwitz et al., Waibel and associates, and others. Although most of these workers expressed amino acid requirements in percentages of the diet, this way of expressing amino acid requirements applies only to the particular set of circumstances used in determining the requirements. In view of the need to change the protein levels with changes in energy content of the diet, and the need for different protein levels during the various stages of turkey growth, a much superior method of expressing amino acid requirements is in terms of percentages of the dietary protein.

Comparisons shown by Scott (1986) demonstrate that the amino acid composition of turkey body proteins is very similar to that of chickens and several other animal species. Furthermore, all evidence indicates that the amino acid composition of the proteins of the eggs of various birds also is similar. Thus, with small variations, the amino acid requirements of turkeys, as percentages of the protein requirements, shown in Table 2.2, are similar to those of chickens. The studies of the above workers indicate only small differences between the requirements of chicks and of poults. The methionine requirement is slightly lower and the lysine requirement is somewhat higher as percentages of the respective protein requirements.

Several recent studies have dealt, not only with the requirement for methionine, but also with the relative biopotencies of the various commercial sources of methionine activity (Noll et al., 1984). Methionine hydroxy analog (free acid) was equivalent to DL-methionine on a molecular basis for both growth and efficiency of feed utilization in Large White turkeys when added to a methionine-low practical diet in several separate experiments.

A number of experiments have been conducted to determine if inorganic sulfate can replace a portion of the methionine-cystine requirement. Although some growth increases have been obtained with sulfate in methionine-deficient diets, these have not been great compared to the responses obtained with added methionine (Sloan and Harms, 1983; Blair, et al., 1986). In the author's own experience (unpublished) calcium sulfate was found to improve

Figure 2.1 Feather depigmentation due to lysine deficiency in a Bronze turkey.

feathering in growing turkeys receiving adequate methionine for normal growth.

One striking difference in the effects of amino acid deficiencies in turkeys versus chickens is the failure of pigmentation in the plummage of bronze turkeys receiving a diet deficient in lysine. This anomaly, discovered in 1946 by Fritz, et al., has been shown by Kratzer and associates (1949, 1950,1956,1958,1959) to be a specific effect of lysine deficiency; it does not occur with deficiencies of any of the other amino acids, and apparently does not occur in chickens having colored plumage. Feather depigmentation in a lysine deficient bronze turkey is shown in Figure 2.1.

Although Kratzer and associates conducted most of the early studies on the essential amino acid requirements of young poults, several other workers also have contributed to this knowledge. Warnick and Anderson (1973) estimated the minimum requirements for essential amino acids, as percentages of the diet to be: arginine, 1.6%; histidine, 0.58%; isoleucine, 1.1%; leucine, 1.86%; lysine, 1.68%; methionine plus cystine, 1.04%; phenylalanine plus tyrosine, 1.8%; threonine, 1.0%; tryptophan, 0.26%; and valine, 1.2%. However, in a later publication (Warnick and Anderson, 1973a) reported, using a 28%-protein starting diet, that growth was improved by 14% when all of the above amino acids were included at 15% above these "minimum" levels. All of these studies have been considered in arriving at the amino acid allowances given in Table 2.2.

In two different experiments, Jackson and Potter (1984) found in Large White turkeys that a 22%-protein growing diet based on corn and soybean meal was deficient in both lysine and valine. Adding leucine or isoleucine caused a further increase in the valine requirement which was found to be in excess of 1.25% of the diet (5.7% of the protein)

Tuttle and Balloun (1974) reported that the lysine requirement of starting poults is approximately 5.4% of the protein, but drops to about 5.1% of the protein after the poults are 8 weeks of age.

Snetsinger et al. (1964) reported the phenylalanine and valine requirements to be 2.5 and 4.6 percent of the protein, respectively (phenylalanine requirement was determined in the presence of plenty of tyrosine).

While relatively meager experimental data are available on the amino acid requirements of modern-day turkeys fed modern-day very high-energy diets, the allowances presented in Table 2.2 have been found to produce excellent growths and efficiencies of feed and protein utilization.

Possible amino acid imbalances

D'Mello (1975) reported that in a diet containing a high level of leucine the level of dietary valine needed increased from a normal requirement of 1.21% to 1.36%. In a turkey starting diet containing 28% protein, these higher levels represent approximately 6.15 and 4.85% of the protein for leucine and valine, respectively. In view of the fact that the leucine content of dehulled soybean meal is approximately 7.8% of the protein and its valine content is only about 5.5% of the protein, it appears possible for an amino acid imbalance to occur under certain conditions. However, no recognition of such an imbalance has ever been reported in turkeys receiving practical diets.

Formulation of diets balanced in energy, protein and amino acids

Parametric analyses using the computer are now employed to determine the particular metabolizable energy and protein levels that are least cost, or to determine the added cost of each increment in energy and protein. It is well established that efficiency of feed utilization improves as the energy (and corresponding protein) level is increased. However, cost of the ration also increases with higher energy-protein levels.

The lowest total cost for turkey production, of course, depends upon many factors. Proper nutrition, however, has by far the greatest effect upon this cost. It is of prime importance therefore that every turkey producer understand and deal with the nutritional factors that will produce best results and lowest feed cost of production throughout the entire growing and finishing periods of each flock.

Because turkeys tend to grow better on the higher energy levels given in Table 2.1, it is not possible to assess, exactly, the cost of using one energy-protein level compared with another at any particular stage of growth. However, a fairly good estimate can be achieved by examining the expected growths and feed conversions when a given set of energy-protein levels are used and then compare these costs with those that would be expected if either a higher or lower energy set of rations were used.

Examples of turkey dietary regimens formulated at least-cost to demonstrate the relationship between energy-protein concentration and economy of turkey production

In order to demonstrate the principle given above, three sets of turkey diets have been formulated below, ranging from a "medium" energy and protein regimen to a high-energy, high-protein series and then to the highest energy and protein levels that are considered to be consistent with commercial practices. Expected growth, efficiency of feed utilization and estimated economy of

Table 2.1. RELATION OF DIETARY PROTEIN REQUIREMENTS TO DIETARY ENERGY AND TO AGE IN TURKEYS

Metabolizable energy	Protein Requirements			
	0-6 wks	6-12	12-16	16 +
Kcal/lb	%	%	%	%
1200	28	22	16.5	---
1250	29	23	17	---
1300	30	24	17.8	
1350	31	25	18.5	14.2
1400	---	26	19	14.8
1450	---	---	20	15.3
1520	---	---	---	16

Note--Turkey poults start well on diets containing 1200 Kcal or more of metabolizable energy per pound; turkey producers should use diets containing as much energy (and corrresponding protein levels) as is economically feasible (see Tables 2.18, 2.19 & 2.20 and 2.33, 2.34 & 2.35).

TABLE 2.2. AMINO ACID ALLOWANCES OF TURKEYS

Essential Amino Acid	Allowances	
	Starting & Growing	Breeding
	Per cent of protein	Per cent of protein
Arginine	5.7	4.5
Histidine	2.1	2.1
Isoleucine	4.0	3.6
Leucine	6.8	3.6
Lysine	5.4 (5.1)*	4.5
Methionine	1.9	1.7
Cystine	1.9	1.6
Phenylalanine	4.0	3.9
Tyrosine	3.5	2.0
Threonine	4.0	3.2
Tryptophan	0.95	0.95
Valine	4.5	4.2
Glycine or Serine	5.0	4.0

*The lysine requirement during the growth period after 8 weeks of age is shown in parentheses.

turkey meat production are given for each regimen.

Shown in Table 2.3 are the expected rates of growth and feed utilization of average turkeys consuming a starting diet containing 1200 Kcal ME and 28% protein during the first six weeks; a diet with 1250 Kcal ME and 23% protein from 6-12 weeks; a diet containing 1300 Kcal and 17.8 % protein from 12-16 weeks and a finishing diet containing 1350 Kcal and 14.5 % protein after 16 weeks of age. These energy-protein levels are considered "medium energy" diets and are those often encountered in the field.

Expected growth and efficiencies of feed utilization of turkeys receiving higher-energy diets are shown in Table 2.4. In this instance diets were used that contained energy levels that were 100 Kcal/kg higher at each stage of growth than were the "medium" energy diets shown in Table 2.3.

As a further comparison, the expected growths and feed conversions of turkeys receiving a very high energy regimen are shown in Table 2.5.

The levels of growth and efficiencies of feed utilization shown in these tables are possible only when the diets contain the levels of amino acids shown in Table 2.2 and are adequate in all vitamins, minerals and trace elements.

In order to illustrate the comparative feed costs of these three dietary regimes, typical feeds have been formulated to the specifications shown in Tables 2.3, 2.4, and 2.5. Two sets of comparative diets are shown below for each stage of growth. These diets are complete in all nutrients required at each stage. For the diets shown in Tables 2.6 through 2.17, wholesale ingredient prices current to the northeastern U. S. were used. In this instance, because of freight costs and for other reasons, diets tend to use higher energy ingredients compared to those often used in the midwestern and western parts of the U. S. These diets almost universally contain corn, dehulled soybean meal, fat, and some fish meal. Diets in the western U. S. may contain milo, 44 %-protein soybean meal, barley, alfalfa meal and other lower-energy ingredients. Therefore, one set of diets has been formulated with corn and dehulled soybean meal (Tables 2.6-2.17), and another set having similar nutrient levels was formulated using milo and non-dehulled (44% protein) soybean meal (Tables 2.21-2.34).

The starting diets given in Tables 2.6 and 2.21 (diets 1200/28) represent the lowest-energy level that can normally assure reasonably satisfactory growth in young poults. The diets shown in Table 2.7 and 2.22 represent moderately high-energy starting diets (diets 1300/30) capable of supporting and promoting maximum growth. The highest-energy starting diets used are shown in Tables 2.8 and 2.23 (1350/31). These are as high in energy as is

Table 2.3. GROWTH AND FEED UTILIZATION IN TURKEYS RECEIVING MEDIUM-ENERGY AND MEDIUM PROTEIN DIETS

AGE	AVERAGE WEIGHTS		FEED CONSUMED		FEED EFFICIENCY
Weeks	Kgm	Lbs	Kgm	Lbs	Feed/Weight
			TOMS		
6	1.7	3.75	2.8	6.1	1.63
12	5.5	12.0	13.2	28.0	2.33
16	9.1	20.0	24.1	53.0	2.65
20	12.5	27.5	40.0	88.0	3.2
22	13.9	30.5	46.4	102	3.35
24	15.2	33.5	55.2	121.5	3.63
			HENS		
6	1.55	3.4	2.6	5.7	1.68
12	4.5	9.9	11.3	24.8	2.5
16	6.5	14.4	18.3	40.3	2.8
18	7.2	15.9	22.3	49.0	3.08

[1] Assuming use of a starting diet (0-6 wks) containing 1200 Kcal ME/lb and 28% protein; a grower # 1 (6-12 wks) with 1250 Kcal/lb and 23% protein; grower # 2 (12-16 wks) with 1300 Kcal ME and 17.8% protein; and a finishing diet with 1350 Kcal ME and 14.5% protein.

Table 2.4. GROWTH AND FEED UTILIZATION IN TURKEYS RECEIVING HIGH-ENERGY AND HIGH-PROTEIN DIETS

AGE	AVERAGE WEIGHTS		FEED CONSUMED		FEED EFFICIENCY
Weeks	Kgm	Lbs	Kgm	Lbs	Feed/Weight
			TOMS		
6	1.75	3.85	2.55	5.6	1.46
12	5.7	12.5	11.8	25.9	2.07
16	9.5	21.0	22.3	49.1	2.34
20	13.1	28.8	37.1	81.7	2.84
22	14.5	32.0	43.0	94.7	2.96
24	15.6	34.3	51.3	112.8	3.29
			HENS		
6	1.55	3.4	2.4	5.35	1.57
12	4.7	10.35	10.4	22.8	2.2
16	6.6	14.5	17.0	37.4	2.58
18	7.4	16.3	20.96	46.1	2.83

[1] Assuming use of a starting diet (0-6 wks) containing 1300 Kcal ME and 30 % protein; a grower # 1 (6-12 wks) with 1350 Kcal ME and 25 % protein; a grower # 2 (12-16 wks) with 1400 Kcal ME and 19 % protein; and a finisher diet with 1450 Kcal and 15.5 % protein. Higher energy diets (higher fat), appropriately balanced with protein and amino acids, will improved efficiency without further improving growth rate.

TABLE 2.5. GROWTH AND FEED UTILIZATION IN TURKEYS RECEIVING HIGHEST ENERGY AND PROTEIN LEVELS COMPATIBLE WITH PRACTICAL TURKEY MANAGEMENT

AGE	AVERAGE WEIGHTS		FEED CONSUMED		FEED EFFICIENCY
Weeks	Kgm	Lbs	Kgm	Lbs	Feed/Weight
			TOMS		
6	1.75	3.85	2.36	5.4	1.35
12	5.7	12.5	11.4	25.0	2.0
16	9.5	21.0	21.8	48.0	2.29
20	13.1	28.8	36.0	79.1	2.75
22	14.5	32.0	41.6	91.5	2.86
24	15.6	34.5	49.4	108.8	3.15
			HENS		
6	1.55	3.4	2.34	5.15	1.51
12	4.7	10.35	10.0	22.0	2.13
16	6.6	14.5	16.3	35.9	2.51
18	7.4	16.3	20.1	44.2	2.71

[1] Assuming use of a starting diet (0-6 wks) containing 1350 Kcal ME/Lb and 31% protein; a grower # 1 diet (6-12 wks) containing 1400 Kcal ME/26 % protein; a grower # 2 diet (12-16 wks) with 1450 Kcal/ lb and 20 % protein; and a finisher diet containing 1520 Kcal/lb and 16 % protein.

usually economical and practical. The comparative economies of these diets will be demonstrated later (Tables 2.18 and 2.33).

Growing and finishing diets of different, increasing energy concentrations under each set of ingredient conditions are shown in Tables 2.9-2.17 for the northeastern U. S., and in Tables 2.21-2.32 for the southwest.[1] All diets are identified in term of their energy/protein ratios.

The wholesale feed costs per pound of feed and per pound of turkey, using these various energy regimens are given for tom turkeys in Tables 2.18, 2.19 and 2.20 for the "northeastern" U.S. and in Tables 2.33, 2.34 and 2.35 for the "southwestern" ingredient conditions.

Even though feed prices in the two areas differed for some of the feedstuffs (Tables 2.6-2.17 vs 2.21-2.32), the middle energy dietary regimen was least-cost in both areas, in term of cost per pound of turkey produced.

These comparisons demonstrate the fallacy of insisting on the use of the lowest-cost feed without considering this cost in relation to the expected efficiency of feed utilization. Conversely, contrary to some beliefs, the highest energy diet is not always the most economical even though the highest energy-protein regimen is the most efficient in terms of pounds of feed per pound of gain in weight.

The relative feed costs per pound of turkey found in these comparisons do not necessarily apply at all times or in all locations. In those areas where corn, dehulled soybean meal, fish meal and fat are very expensive and low-energy ingredients, such as non-dehulled soybean meal, mill byproducts, alfalfa meal, high-fiber sunflower seed oil meal, etc. are cheap, the lowest-energy regimen may not only be the lowest-cost per pound of diet, but also may be the least-cost per pound of turkey.

In the United States, however, it has been well demonstrated under most commercial conditions that the higher-energy regimens are the least-cost in terms of cost of turkey production. The reason for this is that the improvements in feed conversion that occur with relatively high-energy feeds are usually much greater than the increase in cost of these feeds, compared to lower-energy rations.

---

[1] Not all diets in the Southwestern U.S. use milo and non-dehulled soybean meal. This designation is used simply to compare the two types of diets and ingredient prices in different areas of the country.

TABLE 2.6 TURKEY STARTER (CORN) 1200/28, 0-6 WKS

FEED MIX	PRICE	COST	AMOUNT
CORN	4.10	1.42	34.7100
WHEAT MIDDS	3.75	0.83	22.2300
SOYA 48	10.60	2.18	20.5500
FISH MEAL, MENHAD	15.25	1.23	8.0800
BREWERS DRIED GRAINS	5.90	0.31	5.3000
MEAT MEAL 50%	9.00	0.47	5.2400
FEATHER MEAL	11.00	0.33	3.0000
DICAL PHOS	12.75	0.06	0.4900
SALT	2.50	0.01	0.2700
METHIONINE 98.5%	125.00	0.07	0.0580
T-1 PREMIX[1]	305.00	0.15	0.0500
		7.08	99.9780

[1]Premix T-1 provides per kg diet: Vitamins (IU), A=10,000; D_3=3600; E=25; (mg) K=2; B_2=5; B_6=2; B_{12}=0.015; Panto. acid=15; Niacin=80; Biotin=0.1; Folacin=0.5; Choline=900. Minerals (mg), Manganese=75; Zinc=75; Iron=40; Copper=10; Iodine=0.4; Selenium=0.2.

NUTRITIONAL CONTENT

ME	1200.02	CAL/LB
PROTEIN	28.00	%
FAT	4.24	%
FIBER	3.94	%
CALCIUM	1.20	%
PHOS AVAIL	0.75	%
SODIUM	0.18	%
POTASSIUM	0.93	%
METHIONINE	0.54	%
METH+CYS	1.04	%
LYSINE	1.51	%
TRYPTOPHAN	0.32	%
LINOLEIC ACID	1.36	%
DRY MATTER	88.74	%
XANTHOPHYLL	8.68	MG/KG

TABLE 2.7   TURKEY STARTER (CORN) 1300/30, 0-6 WKS

FEED MIX	PRICE	COST	AMOUNT
CORN	4.10	1.75	42.6600
SOYA 48	10.60	2.52	23.7700
BREWERS DRIED GRAINS	5.90	0.88	15.0000
FISH MEAL, MENHAD	15.25	1.42	9.3100
MEAT MEAL 50%	9.00	0.47	5.2400
FEATHER MEAL	11.00	0.33	3.0000
DICAL PHOS	12.75	0.09	0.6700
SALT	2.50	0.01	0.2800
T-1 PREMIX (Table 2.6)	305.00	0.15	0.0500
METHIONINE 98.5%	125.00	0.03	0.0260
		7.65	100.0060

NUTRITIONAL CONTENT

ME	1299.98	CAL/LB
PROTEIN	30.00	%
FAT	4.34	%
FIBER	3.59	%
CALCIUM	1.30	%
PHOS AVAIL	0.80	%
SODIUM	0.19	%
POTASSIUM	0.83	%
METHIONINE	0.58	%
METH+CYS	1.14	%
LYSINE	1.62	%
TRYPTOPHAN	0.36	%
LINOLEIC ACID	1.40	%
DRY MATTER	89.10	%
XANTHOPHYLL	10.66	MG/KG

TABLE 2.8 TURKEY STARTER (CORN) 1350/31, 0-6 WKS

FEED MIX	PRICE	COST	AMOUNT
CORN	4.10	2.02	49.3200
SOYA 48	10.60	3.13	29.5200
FISH MEAL, MENHAD	15.25	2.21	14.4800
FEATHER MEAL	11.00	0.33	3.0000
MEAT MEAL 50%	9.00	0.22	2.4200
DICAL PHOS	12.75	0.12	0.9100
SALT	2.50	0.01	0.3000
T-1 PREMIX (Table 2.6)	305.00	0.15	0.0500
		8.18	100.0000

NUTRITIONAL CONTENT

ME	1350.08	CAL/LB
PROTEIN	31.00	%
FAT	3.78	%
FIBER	2.10	%
CALCIUM	1.30	%
PHOS AVAIL	0.85	%
SODIUM	0.19	%
POTASSIUM	0.95	%
METHIONINE	0.59	%
METH+CYS	1.19	%
LYSINE	1.87	%
TRYPTOPHAN	0.37	%
LINOLEIC ACID	1.11	%
DRY MATTER	88.59	%
XANTHOPHYLL	12.33	MG/KG

TABLE 2.9 TURKEY GROW # 1 (CORN) 1250/23, 6-12 WKS

FEED MIX	PRICE	COST	AMOUNT
CORN	4.10	2.01	49.1400
WHEAT MIDDS	3.75	0.73	19.5800
SOYA 48	10.60	1.18	11.1700
MEAT MEAL 50%	9.00	0.63	7.0500
FISH MEAL, MENHAD	15.25	0.69	4.5000
BREWERS DRIED GRAINS	5.90	0.24	4.0000
FEATHER MEAL	11.00	0.33	3.0000
ALFALFA MEAL, 17%	6.75	0.07	1.0000
SALT	2.50	0.01	0.2600
LYSINE, 78%	150.00	0.29	0.1900
METHIONINE 98.5%	125.00	0.08	0.0640
T-2 PREMIX[1]	190.00	0.09	0.0500
		6.35	100.0040

[1]Premix T-2 provides per kg diet: Vitamins (IU), A=5000; D_3=2000; E=12; (mg) K=2; B_2=4; B_{12}=0.01; Panto. acid=10; Niacin=65; Biotin=0.05; Choline=600. Minerals (mg), Manganese=55; Zinc=65; Iron=25; Copper=10; Iodine=0.4; Selenium=0.2.

NUTRITIONAL CONTENT

ME	1249.95	CAL/LB
PROTEIN	23.00	%
FAT	4.40	%
FIBER	3.82	%
CALCIUM	1.10	%
PHOS AVAIL	0.62	%
SODIUM	0.18	%
POTASSIUM	0.80	%
METHIONINE	0.44	%
METH+CYS	0.87	%
LYSINE	1.23	%
TRYPTOPHAN	0.25	%
LINOLEIC ACID	1.51	%
DRY MATTER	88.18	%
XANTHOPHYLL	14.68	MG/KG

TABLE 2.10 TURKEY GROW # 1 (CORN) 1350/25, 6-12 WKS

FEED MIX	PRICE	COST	AMOUNT
CORN	4.10	2.43	59.2400
SOYA 48	10.60	2.09	19.7400
MEAT MEAL 50%	9.00	0.64	7.0700
FISH MEAL, MENHAD	15.25	0.69	4.5000
BREWERS DRIED GRAINS	5.90	0.24	4.0000
FEATHER MEAL	11.00	0.33	3.0000
ALFALFA MEAL, 17%	6.75	0.07	1.0000
WHEAT MIDDS	3.75	0.03	0.8800
SALT	2.50	0.01	0.2600
LYSINE, 78%	150.00	0.29	0.1900
METHIONINE 98.5%	125.00	0.08	0.0620
T-2 PREMIX (Table 2.9)	190.00	0.09	0.0500
		6.97	99.9200

NUTRITIONAL CONTENT

ME	1350.04	CAL/LB
PROTEIN	25.00	%
FAT	4.01	%
FIBER	2.78	%
CALCIUM	1.10	%
PHOS AVAIL	0.61	%
SODIUM	0.18	%
POTASSIUM	0.83	%
METHIONINE	0.48	%
METH+CYS	0.97	%
LYSINE	1.40	%
TRYPTOPHAN	0.28	%
LINOLEIC ACID	1.38	%
DRY MATTER	88.06	%
XANTHOPHYLL	17.21	MG/KG

TABLE 2.11   TURKEY GROW # 1 (CORN) 1400/26, 6-12 WKS

FEED MIX	PRICE	COST	AMOUNT
CORN	4.10	2.23	54.4200
SOYA 48	10.60	2.44	23.0300
MEAT MEAL 50%	9.00	0.63	7.0100
FISH MEAL, MENHAD	15.25	0.69	4.5000
BREWERS DRIED GRAINS	5.90	0.24	4.0000
FEATHER MEAL	11.00	0.33	3.0000
FAT	11.00	0.27	2.4700
ALFALFA MEAL, 17%	6.75	0.07	1.0000
SALT	2.50	0.01	0.2600
LYSINE, 78%	150.00	0.29	0.1900
METHIONINE 98.5%	125.00	0.09	0.0690
T-2 PREMIX	190.00	0.09	0.0500
		7.37	99.9990

NUTRITIONAL CONTENT

ME	1400.13	CAL/LB
PROTEIN	26.00	%
FAT	6.27	%
FIBER	2.71	%
CALCIUM	1.10	%
PHOS AVAIL	0.61	%
SODIUM	0.18	%
POTASSIUM	0.87	%
METHIONINE	0.50	%
METH+CYS	1.01	%
LYSINE	1.48	%
TRYPTOPHAN	0.29	%
LINOLEIC ACID	1.58	%
DRY MATTER	88.48	%
XANTHOPHYLL	16.01	MG/KG

TABLE 2.12 TURKEY GROW # 2 (CORN) 1300/17.8, 12-16 WKS

FEED MIX	PRICE	COST	AMOUNT
CORN	4.10	2.55	62.0900
WHEAT MIDDS	3.75	0.79	21.0000
MEAT MEAL 50%	9.00	0.62	6.9300
FISH MEAL, MENHAD	15.25	0.83	5.4100
FEATHER MEAL	11.00	0.22	2.0000
BREWERS DRIED GRAINS	5.90	0.06	1.0000
ALFALFA MEAL, 17%	6.75	0.07	1.0000
SALT	2.50	0.01	0.2600
LYSINE, 78%	150.00	0.29	0.1900
T-2 PREMIX	190.00	0.09	0.0500
METHIONINE 98.5%	125.00	0.03	0.0250
		5.55	99.9550

NUTRITIONAL CONTENT

ME	1300.07	CAL/LB
PROTEIN	17.79	%
FAT	4.72	%
FIBER	3.50	%
CALCIUM	1.10	%
PHOS AVAIL	0.63	%
SODIUM	0.18	%
POTASSIUM	0.64	%
METHIONINE	0.34	%
METH+CYS	0.66	%
LYSINE	0.91	%
TRYPTOPHAN	0.18	%
LINOLEIC ACID	1.65	%
DRY MATTER	87.69	%
XANTHOPHYLL	17.93	MG/KG

TABLE 2.13   TURKEY GROW # 2 (CORN) 1400/19, 12-16 WKS

FEED MIX	PRICE	COST	AMOUNT
CORN	4.10	2.98	72.6400
FISH MEAL, MENHAD	15.25	1.08	7.0500
MEAT MEAL 50%	9.00	0.55	6.1200
WHEAT MIDDS	3.75	0.15	4.0200
BREWERS DRIED GRAINS	5.90	0.24	4.0000
FEATHER MEAL	11.00	0.33	3.0000
SOYA 48	10.60	0.18	1.6600
ALFALFA MEAL, 17%	6.75	0.07	1.0000
SALT	2.50	0.01	0.2600
LYSINE, 78%	150.00	0.29	0.1900
T-2 PREMIX	190.00	0.09	0.0500
METHIONINE 98.5%	125.00	0.00	0.0030
		5.95	99.9930

NUTRITIONAL CONTENT

ME	1400.02	CAL/LB
PROTEIN	19.00	%
FAT	4.66	%
FIBER	2.77	%
CALCIUM	1.10	%
PHOS AVAIL	0.61	%
SODIUM	0.18	%
POTASSIUM	0.56	%
METHIONINE	0.36	%
METH+CYS	0.75	%
LYSINE	0.97	%
TRYPTOPHAN	0.20	%
LINOLEIC ACID	1.63	%
DRY MATTER	87.70	%
XANTHOPHYLL	20.56	MG/KG

TABLE 2.14 TURKEY GROW # 2 (CORN) 1450/20, 12-16 WKS

FEED MIX	PRICE	COST	AMOUNT
CORN	4.10	2.87	70.0400
SOYA 48	10.60	0.79	7.4400
MEAT MEAL 50%	9.00	0.66	7.3600
FISH MEAL, MENHAD	15.25	0.69	4.5000
BREWERS DRIED GRAINS	5.90	0.24	4.0000
FEATHER MEAL	11.00	0.33	3.0000
FAT	11.00	0.23	2.1300
ALFALFA MEAL, 17%	6.75	0.07	1.0000
SALT	2.50	0.01	0.2600
LYSINE, 78%	150.00	0.29	0.1900
T-2 PREMIX	190.00	0.09	0.0500
METHIONINE 98.5%	125.00	0.04	0.0320
		6.30	100.0020

NUTRITIONAL CONTENT

ME	1450.02	CAL/LB
PROTEIN	20.00	%
FAT	6.45	%
FIBER	2.57	%
CALCIUM	1.10	%
PHOS AVAIL	0.61	%
SODIUM	0.18	%
POTASSIUM	0.62	%
METHIONINE	0.38	%
METH+CYS	0.79	%
LYSINE	1.03	%
TRYPTOPHAN	0.21	%
LINOLEIC ACID	1.78	%
DRY MATTER	87.99	%
XANTHOPHYLL	19.91	MG/KG

TABLE 2.15   TURKEY FINISHER (CORN) 1350/14.2, 16 WKS+

FEED MIX	PRICE	COST	AMOUNT
CORN	4.10	2.81	68.6000
WHEAT MIDDS	3.75	0.73	19.5100
FISH MEAL, MENHAD	15.25	0.69	4.5000
MEAT MEAL 50%	9.00	0.27	3.0400
BREWERS DRIED GRAINS	5.90	0.12	2.0000
ALFALFA MEAL, 17%	6.75	0.07	1.0000
FAT	11.00	0.06	0.5500
SALT	2.50	0.01	0.3400
LYSINE, 78%	150.00	0.29	0.1900
CALCIUM CARBONATE	1.50	0.00	0.1900
T-2 PREMIX	190.00	0.09	0.0500
FEATHER MEAL	11.00	0.00	0.0000
METHIONINE 98.5%	125.00	0.04	0.0330
		5.18	100.0030

NUTRITIONAL CONTENT

ME	1349.98	CAL/LB
PROTEIN	14.18	%
FAT	5.00	%
FIBER	3.52	%
CALCIUM	0.70	%
PHOS AVAIL	0.40	%
SODIUM	0.18	%
POTASSIUM	0.57	%
METHIONINE	0.31	%
METH+CYS	0.53	%
LYSINE	0.75	%
TRYPTOPHAN	0.16	%
LINOLEIC ACID	1.83	%
DRY MATTER	87.33	%
XANTHOPHYLL	19.55	MG/KG

TABLE 2.16 TURKEY FINISHER (CORN) 1450/15.3, 16 WKS+

FEED MIX	PRICE	COST	AMOUNT
CORN	4.10	3.35	81.8000
MEAT MEAL 50%	9.00	0.57	6.3700
FISH MEAL, MENHAD	15.25	0.79	5.1600
WHEAT MIDDS	3.75	0.11	2.8400
ALFALFA MEAL, 17%	6.75	0.07	1.0000
FEATHER MEAL	11.00	0.11	1.0000
FAT	11.00	0.05	0.4900
SOYA 48	10.60	0.04	0.4200
BREWERS DRIED GRAINS	5.90	0.02	0.4000
SALT	2.50	0.01	0.2800
LYSINE, 78%	150.00	0.29	0.1900
T-2 PREMIX	190.00	0.09	0.0500
		5.51	100.0000

NUTRITIONAL CONTENT

ME	1449.95	CAL/LB
PROTEIN	15.30	%
FAT	5.00	%
FIBER	2.35	%
CALCIUM	1.00	%
PHOS AVAIL	0.56	%
SODIUM	0.18	%
POTASSIUM	0.53	%
METHIONINE	0.30	%
METH+CYS	0.59	%
LYSINE	0.79	%
TRYPTOPHAN	0.16	%
LINOLEIC ACID	1.72	%
DRY MATTER	87.24	%
XANTHOPHYLL	22.85	MG/KG

TABLE 2.17 TURKEY FINISHER (CORN) 1520/16, 16 WKS+

FEED MIX	PRICE	COST	AMOUNT
CORN	4.10	3.41	83.1700
FISH MEAL, MENHAD	15.25	1.20	7.8700
FEATHER MEAL	11.00	0.33	3.0000
MEAT MEAL 50%	9.00	0.21	2.3500
FAT	11.00	0.22	2.0400
ALFALFA MEAL, 17%	6.75	0.07	1.0000
SALT	2.50	0.01	0.3300
LYSINE, 78%	150.00	0.29	0.1900
T-2 PREMIX	190.00	0.09	0.0500
		5.83	100.0000

NUTRITIONAL CONTENT

ME	1520.05	CAL/LB
PROTEIN	16.00	%
FAT	6.33	%
FIBER	2.06	%
CALCIUM	0.73	%
PHOS AVAIL	0.44	%
SODIUM	0.18	%
POTASSIUM	0.47	%
METHIONINE	0.32	%
METH+CYS	0.68	%
LYSINE	0.82	%
TRYPTOPHAN	0.17	%
LINOLEIC ACID	1.86	%
DRY MATTER	87.39	%
XANTHOPHYLL	23.19	MG/KG

TABLE 2.18 FEED COSTS PER POUND OF TURKEY USING MEDIUM ENERGY
DIETARY REGIMEN

Weeks	Diet	Expected feed conversion	Cost per pound of feed	Cost per pound of turkey	Growth increment for period	Total cost per turkey
		feed/wt	$	$	pounds	$
		TOMS				
0-6	(TABLE 2.6)	1.63	.0708	.115	3.75	.431
6-12	(TABLE 2.9)	2.33	.0635	.148	8.25	1.221
12-16	(TABLE 2.12)	2.65	.0555	.147	8.00	1.176
16-20	(TABLE 2.15)	3.2	.0518	.1658	7.50	1.244
20-22	(")	3.35	.0518	.174	3.00	.522
22-24	(")	3.63	.0518	.1880	3.00	.564
	Totals	3.63			33.50	5.159

Feed cost per pound of turkey = $ 0.154

TABLE 2.19. FEED COSTS PER POUND OF TURKEY USING A NORTHEASTERN HIGHER-ENERGY DIETARY REGIMEN

Weeks	Diet	Expected feed conversions	Cost per pound of feed	Cost per pound of turkey	Growth increment for period	Total cost per turkey
		feed/wt	$	$	pounds	$
			TOMS			
0-6	(TABLE 2.7)	1.46	.0765	.112	3.85	.431
6-12	(TABLE 2.10)	2.07	.0697	.144	8.65	1.246
12-16	(TABLE 2.13)	2.34	.0595	.139	8.50	1.182
16-20	(TABLE 2.16)	2.84	.0551	.156	7.80	1.217
20-22	(" ")	2.96	.0551	.163	3.20	.522
22-24	(" ")	3.29	.0551	.181	2.30	.416
Totals		3.29			34.30	5.014

Feed cost per lb of turkey = $ 0.146

TABLE 2.20. FEED COSTS PER POUND OF TURKEY USING A VERY
HIGH-ENERGY NORTHEASTERN DIETARY REGIMEN

Weeks	Diet	Expected feed conversions	Cost per pound of feed	Cost per pound of turkey	Growth increment for period	Total cost per turkey
		feed/wt	$	$	pounds	$
0-6	(TABLE 2.8)	1.35	.0818	.110	3.85	.425
6-12	(TABLE 2.11)	2.00	.0737	.1474	8.65	1.275
12-16	(TABLE 2.14)	2.29	.063	.1443	8.50	1.226
16-20	(TABLE 2.17)	2.75	.0583	.1603	7.80	1.250
20-22	(" ")	2.86	.0583	.1667	3.20	.533
22-24	(" ")	3.15	.0583	.1836	2.50	.459
Totals		3.15			34.5	5.167

Feed cost per pound of turkey = $ 0.150

TABLE 2.21   TURKEY STARTER (MILO) 1200/28, 0-6 WKS

FEED MIX	PRICE	COST	AMOUNT
MILO	3.20	1.33	41.7000
SOYBEAN MEAL, 44%	9.00	1.89	21.0000
WHEAT MIDDS	3.50	0.60	17.2700
FISH MEAL, MENHAD	15.40	1.50	9.7200
MEAT MEAL 50%	10.50	0.60	5.7600
FEATHER MEAL	11.00	0.33	3.0000
ALFALFA MEAL, 17%	4.00	0.04	1.0000
SALT	2.50	0.01	0.2500
DICAL PHOS	12.75	0.02	0.1400
METHIONINE 98.5%	125.00	0.11	0.0900
T-1 PREMIX (Table 2.6)	305.00	0.15	0.0500
		6.59	99.9800

NUTRITIONAL CONTENT

ME	1199.83	CAL/LB
PROTEIN	28.01	%
FAT	3.71	%
FIBER	3.96	%
CALCIUM	1.30	%
PHOS AVAIL	0.75	%
SODIUM	0.18	%
POTASSIUM	0.94	%
METHIONINE	0.56	%
METH+CYS	1.04	%
LYSINE	1.51	%
TRYPTOPHAN	0.31	%
LINOLEIC ACID	0.92	%
DRY MATTER	89.79	%
XANTHOPHYLL	2.40	MG/KG

TABLE 2.22 TURKEY STARTER (MILO) 1300/30, 0-6 WKS

FEED MIX	PRICE	COST	AMOUNT
MILO	3.20	1.59	49.6000
SOYBEAN MEAL, 44%	9.00	2.57	28.5000
FISH MEAL, MENHAD	15.40	1.91	12.3900
MEAT MEAL 50%	10.50	0.39	3.7100
FEATHER MEAL	11.00	0.33	3.0000
ALFALFA MEAL, 17%	4.00	0.04	1.0000
FAT	11.00	0.08	0.7600
DICAL PHOS	12.75	0.07	0.5700
SALT	2.50	0.01	0.2900
METHIONINE 98.5%	125.00	0.09	0.0730
T-1 PREMIX (Table 2.6)	305.00	0.15	0.0500
		7.23	99.9430

NUTRITIONAL CONTENT

ME	1299.95	CAL/LB
PROTEIN	30.01	%
FAT	4.00	%
FIBER	3.17	%
CALCIUM	1.30	%
PHOS AVAIL	0.80	%
SODIUM	0.19	%
POTASSIUM	0.93	%
METHIONINE	0.60	%
METH+CYS	1.14	%
LYSINE	1.71	%
TRYPTOPHAN	0.35	%
LINOLEIC ACID	0.80	%
DRY MATTER	90.12	%
XANTHOPHYLL	2.40	MG/KG

TABLE 2.23   TURKEY STARTER (MILO) 1350/31, 0-6 WKS

FEED MIX	PRICE	COST	AMOUNT
MILO	3.20	1.41	44.1000
SOYBEAN MEAL, 44%	9.00	2.76	30.7000
FISH MEAL, MENHAD	15.40	2.31	15.0000
FAT	11.00	0.35	3.1600
FEATHER MEAL	11.00	0.33	3.0000
MEAT MEAL 50%	10.50	0.18	1.7600
ALFALFA MEAL, 17%	4.00	0.04	1.0000
DICAL PHOS	12.75	0.12	0.9300
SALT	2.50	0.01	0.3100
T-1 PREMIX (Table 2.6)	305.00	0.15	0.0500
METHIONINE 98.5%	125.00	0.03	0.0260
		7.70	100.0360

NUTRITIONAL CONTENT

ME	1349.95	CAL/LB
PROTEIN	30.99	%
FAT	6.30	%
FIBER	3.18	%
CALCIUM	1.30	%
PHOS AVAIL	0.85	%
SODIUM	0.19	%
POTASSIUM	0.95	%
METHIONINE	0.59	%
METH+CYS	1.15	%
LYSINE	1.84	%
TRYPTOPHAN	0.37	%
LINOLEIC ACID	1.04	%
DRY MATTER	90.46	%
XANTHOPHYLL	2.40	MG/KG

TABLE 2.24 TURKEY GROW # 1 (MILO) 1250/23, 6-12 WKS

FEED MIX	PRICE	COST	AMOUNT
MILO	3.20	1.46	45.7000
WHEAT MIDDS	3.50	0.61	17.3700
FISH MEAL, MENHAD	15.40	1.54	10.0000
BARLEY	2.50	0.25	10.0000
SOYBEAN MEAL, 44%	9.00	0.83	9.2000
MEAT MEAL 50%	10.50	0.38	3.6400
FEATHER MEAL	11.00	0.33	3.0000
ALFALFA MEAL, 17%	4.00	0.04	1.0000
SALT	2.50	0.01	0.2800
T-2 PREMIX	190.00	0.09	0.0500
METHIONINE 98.5%	125.00	0.05	0.0380
		5.59	100.2780

NUTRITIONAL CONTENT

ME	1249.62	CAL/LB
PROTEIN	23.12	%
FAT	3.72	%
FIBER	3.94	%
CALCIUM	1.04	%
PHOS AVAIL	0.60	%
SODIUM	0.18	%
POTASSIUM	0.74	%
METHIONINE	0.44	%
METH+CYS	0.86	%
LYSINE	1.17	%
TRYPTOPHAN	0.26	%
LINOLEIC ACID	1.00	%
DRY MATTER	89.77	%
XANTHOPHYLL	2.39	MG/KG

TABLE 2.25   TURKEY GROW # 1 (MILO) 1350/25, 6-12 WKS

FEED MIX	PRICE	COST	AMOUNT
MILO	3.20	2.06	64.3000
SOYBEAN MEAL, 44%	9.00	1.46	16.2000
FISH MEAL, MENHAD	15.40	1.54	10.0000
MEAT MEAL 50%	10.50	0.51	4.8400
FEATHER MEAL	11.00	0.33	3.0000
ALFALFA MEAL, 17%	4.00	0.04	1.0000
FAT	11.00	0.03	0.2700
SALT	2.50	0.01	0.2600
T-2 PREMIX	190.00	0.09	0.0500
METHIONINE 98.5%	125.00	0.04	0.0350
		6.11	99.9550

NUTRITIONAL CONTENT

ME	1350.01	CAL/LB
PROTEIN	25.01	%
FAT	3.71	%
FIBER	2.73	%
CALCIUM	1.16	%
PHOS AVAIL	0.65	%
SODIUM	0.18	%
POTASSIUM	0.74	%
METHIONINE	0.47	%
METH+CYS	0.93	%
LYSINE	1.29	%
TRYPTOPHAN	0.27	%
LINOLEIC ACID	0.85	%
DRY MATTER	89.94	%
XANTHOPHYLL	2.40	MG/KG

TABLE 2.26 TURKEY GROW # 1 (MILO) 1400/26, 6-12 WKS

FEED MIX	PRICE.	COST	AMOUNT
MILO	3.20	1.83	57.2000
SOYBEAN MEAL, 44%	9.00	1.81	20.1000
FISH MEAL, MENHAD	15.40	1.54	10.0000
MEAT MEAL 50%	10.50	0.50	4.7300
FAT	11.00	0.37	3.3400
FEATHER MEAL	11.00	0.33	3.0000
ALFALFA MEAL, 17%	4.00	0.04	1.0000
SALT	2.50	0.01	0.2700
DICAL PHOS	12.75	0.03	0.2400
T-2 PREMIX	190.00	0.09	0.0500
METHIONINE 98.5%	125.00	0.05	0.0420
		6.60	99.9720

NUTRITIONAL CONTENT

ME	1400.16	CAL/LB
PROTEIN	26.00	%
FAT	6.60	%
FIBER	2.82	%
CALCIUM	1.2010	%
PHOS AVAIL	0.70	%
SODIUM	0.18	%
POTASSIUM	0.79	%
METHIONINE	0.49	%
METH+CYS	0.97	%
LYSINE	1.39	%
TRYPTOPHAN	0.29	%
LINOLEIC ACID	1.16	%
DRY MATTER	90.30	%
XANTHOPHYLL	2.40	MG/KG

TABLE 2.27   TURKEY GROW # 2 (MILO) 1300/17.8, 12-16 WKS

FEED MIX	PRICE	COST	AMOUNT
MILO	3.20	1.81	56.5000
WHEAT MIDDS	3.50	0.60	17.2600
BARLEY	2.50	0.25	10.0000
FISH MEAL, MENHAD	15.40	1.54	10.0000
MEAT MEAL 50%	10.50	0.32	3.0400
SOYBEAN MEAL, 44%	9.00	0.16	1.8000
ALFALFA MEAL, 17%	4.00	0.04	1.0000
SALT	2.50	0.01	0.3000
T-2 PREMIX	190.00	0.09	0.0500
METHIONINE 98.5%	125.00	0.04	0.0350
		4.87	99.9850

NUTRITIONAL CONTENT

ME	1299.85	CAL/LB
PROTEIN	18.07	%
FAT	3.83	%
FIBER	3.67	%
CALCIUM	0.94	%
PHOS AVAIL	0.55	%
SODIUM	0.18	%
POTASSIUM	0.60	%
METHIONINE	0.39	%
METH+CYS	0.65	%
LYSINE	0.92	%
TRYPTOPHAN	0.21	%
LINOLEIC ACID	1.09	%
DRY MATTER	89.66	%
XANTHOPHYLL	2.40	MG/KG

TABLE 2.28   TURKEY GROW # 2 (MILO) 1400/19, 12-16 WKS

FEED MIX	PRICE	COST	AMOUNT
MILO	3.20	2.23	69.6000
FISH MEAL, MENHAD	15.40	1.54	10.0000
BARLEY	2.50	0.25	10.0000
SOYBEAN MEAL, 44%	9.00	0.36	4.0000
MEAT MEAL 50%	10.50	0.35	3.3500
FEATHER MEAL	11.00	0.11	1.0000
ALFALFA MEAL, 17%	4.00	0.04	1.0000
SALT	2.50	0.01	0.2900
FAT	11.00	0.02	0.2000
LYSINE, 78%	150.00	0.09	0.0580
T-2 PREMIX	190.00	0.09	0.0500
		5.09	99.5480

NUTRITIONAL CONTENT

ME	1401.67	CAL/LB
PROTEIN	18.70	%
FAT	3.69	%
FIBER	2.71	%
CALCIUM	0.97	%
PHOS AVAIL	0.55	%
SODIUM	0.18	%
POTASSIUM	0.54	%
METHIONINE	0.36	%
METH+CYS	0.68	%
LYSINE	0.97	%
TRYPTOPHAN	0.21	%
LINOLEIC ACID	0.94	%
DRY MATTER	89.89	%
XANTHOPHYLL	2.41	MG/KG

TABLE 2.29   TURKEY GROW # 2 (MILO) 1450/20, 12-16 WKS

FEED MIX	PRICE	COST	AMOUNT
MILO	3.20	2.03	63.5000
FISH MEAL, MENHAD	15.40	1.54	10.0000
BARLEY	2.50	0.25	10.0000
SOYBEAN MEAL, 44%	9.00	0.64	7.1000
MEAT MEAL 50%	10.50	0.34	3.2700
FAT	11.00	0.33	2.9800
FEATHER MEAL	11.00	0.22	2.0000
ALFALFA MEAL, 17%	4.00	0.04	1.0000
SALT	2.50	0.01	0.2900
T-2 PREMIX	190.00	0.09	0.0500
LYSINE, 78%	150.00	0.03	0.0210
METHIONINE 98.5%	125.00	0.00	0.0040
		5.53	100.2150

NUTRITIONAL CONTENT

ME	1448.97	CAL/LB
PROTEIN	20.15	%
FAT	6.32	%
FIBER	2.77	%
CALCIUM	0.97	%
PHOS AVAIL	0.55	%
SODIUM	0.18	%
POTASSIUM	0.58	%
METHIONINE	0.38	%
METH+CYS	0.75	%
LYSINE	1.02	%
TRYPTOPHAN	0.23	%
LINOLEIC ACID	1.21	%
DRY MATTER	90.22	%
XANTHOPHYLL	2.39	MG/KG

TABLE 2.30   TURKEY FINISHER (MILO) 1350/14.5, 16 WKS+

FEED MIX	PRICE	COST	AMOUNT
MILO	3.20	1.93	60.2000
WHEAT MIDDS	3.50	0.56	15.9200
BARLEY	2.50	0.25	10.0000
FISH MEAL, MENHAD	15.40	1.15	7.5000
MEAT MEAL 50%	10.50	0.26	2.4800
FAT	11.00	0.16	1.4200
SOYBEAN MEAL, 44%	9.00	0.10	1.1000
ALFALFA MEAL, 17%	4.00	0.04	1.0000
SALT	2.50	0.01	0.3300
T-2 PREMIX	190.00	0.09	0.0500
METHIONINE 98.5%	125.00	0.01	0.0120
		4.56	100.0120

NUTRITIONAL CONTENT

ME	1350.04	CAL/LB
PROTEIN	16.08	%
FAT	5.00	%
FIBER	3.56	%
CALCIUM	0.74	%
PHOS AVAIL	0.45	%
SODIUM	0.18	%
POTASSIUM	0.56	%
METHIONINE	0.32	%
METH+CYS	0.55	%
LYSINE	0.76	%
TRYPTOPHAN	0.18	%
LINOLEIC ACID	1.26	%
DRY MATTER	89.68	%
XANTHOPHYLL	2.40	MG/KG

TABLE 2.31 TURKEY FINISHER (MILO) 1450/15.5, 16 WKS+

FEED MIX	PRICE	COST	AMOUNT
MILO	3.20	2.35	73.4000
BARLEY	2.50	0.25	10.0000
FISH MEAL, MENHAD	15.40	1.15	7.5000
SOYBEAN MEAL, 44%	9.00	0.28	3.1000
MEAT MEAL 50%	10.50	0.30	2.8300
FAT	11.00	0.19	1.7300
ALFALFA MEAL, 17%	4.00	0.04	1.0000
SALT	2.50	0.01	0.3200
LYSINE, 78%	150.00	0.10	0.0690
T-2 PREMIX	190.00	0.09	0.0500
METHIONINE, 98.6%	125.00	0.02	0.0190
		4.79	100.0180

NUTRITIONAL CONTENT

ME	1450.09	CAL/LB
PROTEIN	15.98	%
FAT	5.00	%
FIBER	2.68	%
CALCIUM	0.77	%
PHOS AVAIL	0.45	%
SODIUM	0.18	%
POTASSIUM	0.50	%
METHIONINE	0.33	%
METH+CYS	0.58	%
LYSINE	0.80	%
TRYPTOPHAN	0.18	%
LINOLEIC ACID	1.15	%
DRY MATTER	89.88	%
XANTHOPHYLL	2.40	MG/KG

TABLE 2.32 TURKEY FINISHER (MILO) 1520/16, 16 WKS+

FEED MIX	PRICE	COST	AMOUNT
MILO	3.20	2.29	71.5000
BARLEY	2.50	0.25	10.0000
FISH MEAL, MENHAD	15.40	1.15	7.5000
FAT	11.00	0.50	4.5800
MEAT MEAL 50%	10.50	0.31	2.9200
FEATHER MEAL	11.00	0.22	2.0000
ALFALFA MEAL, 17%	4.00	0.04	1.0000
SOYBEAN MEAL, 44%	9.00	0.04	0.4000
SALT	2.50	0.01	0.3200
LYSINE, 78%	150.00	0.26	0.1700
T-2 PREMIX	190.00	0.09	0.0500
METHIONINE, 98.5%	125.00	0.03	0.0230
		5.19	100.4630

NUTRITIONAL CONTENT

ME	1517.77	CAL/LB
PROTEIN	16.33	%
FAT	7.80	%
FIBER	2.49	%
CALCIUM	0.77	%
PHOS AVAIL	0.45	%
SODIUM	0.18	%
POTASSIUM	0.45	%
METHIONINE	0.32	%
METH+CYS	0.63	%
LYSINE	0.82	%
TRYPTOPHAN	0.17	%
LINOLEIC ACID	1.45	%
DRY MATTER	90.24	%
XANTHOPHYLL	2.39	MG/KG

TABLE 2.33. FEED COSTS PER POUND OF TURKEY USING A SOUTHWESTERN MEDIUM-ENERGY (MILO) DIETARY REGIMEN

WEEKS	Diet	Expected feed conversion	Cost per pound of feed	Cost per pound of turkey	Growth increment for period	Total cost per turkey
		feed/wt	$	$	pounds	$
			TOMS			
0-6	(Table 2.21)	1.63	.0659	.1074	3.75	.403
6-12	(Table 2.24)	2.33	.0559	.1302	8.25	1.074
12-16	(Table 2.27)	2.65	.0487	.1290	8.00	1.032
16-20	(Table 2.30)	3.20	.0456	.1460	7.50	1.095
20-22	(" ")	3.35	.0456	.1528	3.00	.458
22-24	(" ")	3.63	.0456	.1655	3.00	.497
Totals		3.63			33.50	4.559

Feed cost per pound of turkey = $ 0.136

TABLE 2.34. FEED COST PER POUND OF TURKEY USING A HIGHER-ENERGY SOUTHWESTERN (MILO) DIETARY REGIMEN

Weeks	Diet	Expected feed conversions	Cost per pound of feed	Cost per pound of turkey	Growth increment for period	Total cost per turkey
		feed/wt	$	$	pounds	$
		TOMS				
0-6	(TABLE 2.22)	1.46	.0723	.1055	3.85	.406
6-12	(Table 2.25)	2.07	.0611	.1265	8.65	1.109
12-16	(Table 2.28)	2.34	.0509	.1265	8.5	1.012
16-20	(Table 2.31)	2.84	.0479	.1360	7.8	1.061
20-22	(" ")	2.96	.0479	.1418	3.2	.454
22-24	(" ")	3.29	.0479	.1576	2.3	.362
Totals		3.29			34.3	4.404

Feed cost per pound of turkey = $ 0.128

TABLE 2.35. FEED COST PER POUND OF TURKEY USING A VERY
HIGH-ENERGY SOUTHWESTERN (MILO) DIETARY REGIMEN

Weeks	Diet	Expected feed conversion	Cost per pound of feed	Cost per pound of turkey	Growth increment for period	Total cost per turkey
		feed/wt	$	$	pounds	$
0-6	(Table 2.23)	1.35	.0770	.1040	3.85	.400
6-12	(Table 2.26)	2.00	.0660	.1320	8.65	1.142
12-16	(Table 2.29)	2.29	.0553	.1266	8.5	1.076
16-20	(Table 2.32)	2.75	.0519	.1427	7.8	1.113
20-22	(" ")	2.86	.0519	.1484	3.2	.475
22-24	(" ")	3.15	.0519	.1635	2.5	.409
Totals		3.15			34.5	4.615

Feed cost per pound of turkey = $ 0.134

As shown in these comparisons, however, this effect plateaus at a certain energy level such that the cost increase is then greater than the further improvement in efficiency of feed utilization.

The presence of a high fat content in the higher-energy growing and finishing diets contributes greatly to this economy of turkey production because it reduces the "heat increment" of the diet. This is very important, particularly in hot weather, such as exists especially in August and September, two important months of the late growing and finishing periods in many turkey flocks.

In 1958, Jowsey, Blakely and MacGregor reported that the feeding of fat, up to 10% tallow, in a 16%-protein growing ration, significantly improved growth, efficiency of feed utilization and market finish in market turkeys. This was confirmed by Essary, Potter and Leighton with 8% added fat. Touchburn and Naber (1969) and Jensen and associates (1970, 1973, 1974) showed that this "extra-caloric" effect of fat improved all parameters above those that could be accounted for simply on the basis of the higher ME value of fat as compared to carbohydrate. They found that the effect of fat occurred only in nutrionally-complete diets and plateaued at a level of approximately 8% fat. Although pelleting turkey grower diets improves results when the diets are low in fat, Jensen and Falen (1973) found that an unpelleted growing ration containing 6% fat produced maximum results which were not improved by pelleting the diet.

In some intensive studies of fat levels in turkey diets, Sell and Associates (1983,1986) fed turkeys graded levels of tallow compared to similar levels of an animal-vegetable blended fat (AV fat). In one study, comparing the effects of added fat at various stages of growth, improvements in efficiency of feed utilization due to the added fat were found to increase as the turkeys grew older (i.e. were greater during the late growing stages compared to the starting and early growth periods). Estimates of the ME values of these fats indicated that tallow contained 6808 kcal ME per kg at two weeks of age and 8551 kcal per kg at 8 weeks of age. The AV fat appeared to contain 7114 kcal ME at two weeks and 8924 kcal ME per kg at 8 weeks of age. Fatty acid analyses indicated that absorption and utilization of palmitic and stearic acids improved as the turkeys grew older. Also the fatty-acid-binding proteins (FABP) of the intestines increased markedly as the turkey grew older. Dietary fat levels had no effect upon the levels of FABP.

A review of experiments indicates that turkey growers #2 and finisher feeds should contain at least 5% fat. This appears to be the minimum level that will bring about this desirable reduction in the "heat increment".

For a further explanation of the "heat increment" (the associative dynamic action of fats) the reader is referred to the basic textbook, "Nutrition of the Chicken" by Scott, Nesheim and Young (pp. 32-33).

Energy, protein and amino acid requirements of breeding trukeys

Studies on energy and protein levels required by breeding turkeys (Atkinson, et al., Ferket, et al., Harms, et al., Jensen et al.,Moran, et al., Rosebrough, et al., Waibel, and others) show that turkey hens can adapt to wide variations in dietary energy and protein levels. Energy levels as low as 1100 Kcal. metabolizable energy in summer have been shown to produce as good egg production as that obtained with energy levels up to 1350 Kcal. per pound of diet. Maintenance of body weight, however, was found to require a diet with about 1300-1350 Kcal. ME/lb. in a cool climate in the winter.

Experiments on protein requirements indicate that in a cool climate as little as 13% protein is sufficient together with an energy level of 1300 Kcal. ME/lb of diet as long as the lysine and sulfur amino acids are present in adequate amounts.

The National Research Council (NRC) recommendations presented in the 1984 bulletin entitled Nutrient Requirements of Poultry indicate an energy level for breeding turkeys of 2900 Kcal ME per kilogram (1318 Kcal/lb) of diet together with a protein level of 14%. The NRC recommendations for lysine of 0.6% and of total sulfur amino acids of only 0.4% are lower than the values found by Atkinson, et al. (1974) who indicated that the lysine requirement approximated 0.85% and the methionine plus cystine requirement was at least 0.6% of the diet under Texas conditions.

It is obvious that the energy requirement of a breeding turkey hen is that amount of metabolizable energy needed each day for optimum maintenance of a physically fit body and for necessary activity plus the energy needed for the production of a good, hatchable egg.

It is not possible to present these requirements simply as amounts per pound of diet because many factors may influence these requirements and the feed intake. The major factors influencing energy requirements are body weight and environmental temperature.

A smaller hen naturally requires less energy per day than a larger hen. This difference is not very important because the smaller hen will naturally consume less of a given feed than is consumed by a larger hen.

Environmental temperature, however, is very important. Breeding turkeys housed at an average temperature 60 degrees F.(15 degrees

C.) will require about 10 % more energy than the same turkeys would require at 78 degrees F.(25 degrees C.)

In view of this, it is desirable to determine the daily energy and protein requirements of breeding turkeys of different body weights and then to relate this to the energy contents of the breeding diets and to the average ambient temperatures to be encountered.

The author (Scott, 1986) has calculated the maintenance energy requirement of a turkey hen weighing 7.5 kilograms (16.5 lbs.) with sedentary activity (in close confinement) at 70 degrees F. (21 degrees C.) to be 618 Kcal. ME/day.

Turkey egg weights range from about 80 to 100 grams. Marion (1974) reported that at 35 weeks of age a commercial flock of breeding turkeys produced eggs averaging 82.4 grams which contained 9.8% shell, 26.4% yolk, and 63.8% albumin. At 51 weeks of age, these parameters had changed so that the egg weight averaged 97.6 grams, 8.4% shell, 30.3% yolk and 61.1% albumin. The yolk contained 46.6% moisture, 16.33% protein and 36.17% fat. The albumin contained 87.3% moisture and 9.49% protein. These values are of importance in calculating the absolute energy and protein requirements of turkey breeding hens in terms of the amounts per hen per day.

According to the USDA (1976), a medium-sized turkey egg weighing 80 grams contains 173 Kcal. of energy and 13.5 grams of protein.

Thus, the daily energy needs of the above turkey hen for maximum egg production would be 618 + 173 = 791 Kcal. ME. Accordingly, if this hen were fed a diet containing the NRC recommended level of 2900 Kcal ME/kg, she would need to consume 791 divided by 2900 = 0.273 kilograms (or 0.6 pounds) of this feed per day to obtain her necessary energy.

According to the author's previous calculations (Scott, 1986) this adult turkey hen requires 6.42 grams of protein per day simply for maintenance of tissue losses due to "wear and tear".

Thus, the daily protein needs of the above hen for maximum egg production would be 6.42 + 13.5 = 19.92 grams.

The average efficiency of dietary protein utilization with common poultry feeds is about 55%.

In order to supply the body and egg needs for protein, therefore, the dietary intake of protein must be 19.92 divided by 0.55 = 36.22 grams per hen per day.

Assuming that the feed intake of 273 grams is consumed to meet the energy requirements, this feed must contain 36.22 divided by

273 = 13.3% protein in order to meet the protein requirements for maximum production--and this feed must be adequate in all essential amino acids and other nutrients.

If, however, the average temperature is 30 degrees C.(85 degrees F), the energy requirement for maintenance would be approximately 10% less, or only about 555 Kcal. Adding the 173 Kcal content of the egg would make a total energy need of 728 Kcal ME/hen/day.

If the same hen is fed the diet containing 2900 Kcal ME/kg, she would need to consume only 0.25 kg or 0.55 lb/hen/day to obtain her energy needs.

To provide her protein requirement, this diet would need to contain 36.22 divided by 250 = 14.5% protein. Due to the fact that somewhat smaller hens would consume even less feed for their energy needs yet produce an almost comparable egg, the protein requirement, as percent of the diet, for these hens would be still higher.

Because it is almost impossible to formulate diets to an exact protein level at all times, at least a 10% margin of safety appears to be warranted, especially in the diet of turkey breeders wherein the egg production cycle is of short duration and the cost of production, and thus the price of the poults, is high.

The energy and protein recommendations, given in Table 2.36, for breeding turkey hens, represent generous margins of safety over minimum requirements.

Experiments with breeding toms (Ferket and Moran,1985; Moran et al.,1983) indicate that best reproductive results are achieved when the toms receive a relatively low energy, low protein diet similar to the finisher diet given in Table 2.15.

However, too much fiber in the tom breeding diet causes difficulties in obtaining semen uncontaminated with feces for use in artificial insemination.

Amino acid requirements of breeding turkeys

Little research has been conducted on the amino acid requirements of adult turkeys. Practical experience indicates that the amino acid levels given in Table 2.2 are adequate for breeding turkey toms and hens as percentages of the respective protein allowances.

An example of a least-cost turkey breeding ration for summer is presented in Table 2.37. A turkey breeder ration for winter is shown in Table 2.38. These rations contain the levels of protein, energy and amino acids discussed in the sections above.

TABLE 2.36. ENERGY AND PROTEIN ALLOWANCES FOR BREEDING TURKEY HENS.

Metabolizable energy of the diet		Suggested protein allowances	
		Winter	Summer
Kcalories per		% of diet	% of diet
Kg	Lb		
2640	1200	14.5	15.5
2750	1250	15.0	16.0
2860	1300	15.5	16.5
2970	1350	16.0	17.0

These values represent generous margins of safety over minimum requirements (see text).

TABLE 2.37   TURKEY BREEDER RATION FOR SUMMER

FEED MIX	PRICE	COST	AMOUNT
CORN	3.50	2.12	60.7100
SOYA 48	9.90	1.11	11.2200
WHEAT MIDDS	4.00	0.40	10.0000
CALCIUM CARBONATE	1.33	0.07	5.5000
CORN GLUTEN FEED	4.10	0.20	5.0000
FISH MEAL, MENHAD	17.50	0.52	3.0000
BREWERS YEAST	41.00	0.82	2.0000
DICAL PHOS	10.20	0.10	1.0200
ALFALFA MEAL, 17%	6.10	0.06	1.0000
SALT	4.00	0.01	0.3200
T-1 PREMIX (Table 2.6)	305.00	0.15	0.0500
LYSINE, 78%	140.00	0.08	0.0560
METHIONINE 98.5%	125.00	0.03	0.0240
		5.66	100.0000

NUTRITIONAL CONTENT

ME	1258.10	CAL/LB
PROTEIN	16.00	%
FAT	3.41	%
FIBER	3.563.13	%
CALCIUM	2.50	%
PHOS AVAIL	0.45	%
SODIUM	0.18	%
POTASSIUM	0.67	%
METHIONINE	0.32	%
METH+CYS	0.58	%
LYSINE	0.80	%
TRYPTOPHAN	0.20	%
LINOLEIC ACID	1.45	%
DRY MATTER	88.27	%
XANTHOPHYLL	17.57	MG/KG

TABLE 2.38 TURKEY BREEDER RATION FOR WINTER

FEED MIX	PRICE	COST	AMOUNT
CORN	3.50	2.57	73.5300
SOYA 48	9.90	1.19	12.0200
CALCIUM CARBONATE	1.33	0.07	4.9500
FISH MEAL, MENHAD	17.50	0.52	3.0000
MEAT MEAL 50%	10.50	0.27	2.5500
BREWERS YEAST	41.00	0.82	2.0000
ALFALFA MEAL, 17%	6.10	0.06	1.0000
DICAL PHOS	10.20	0.05	0.4900
SALT	4.00	0.01	0.2900
T-1 PREMIX (Table 2.6)	305.00	0.15	0.0500
METHIONINE 98.5%	125.00	0.02	0.0150
		5.70	99.9950

NUTRITIONAL CONTENT

ME	1349.96	CAL/LB
PROTEIN	16.00	%
FAT	3.61	%
FIBER	2.21	%
CALCIUM	2.46	%
PHOS AVAIL	0.45	%
SODIUM	0.15	%
POTASSIUM	0.65	%
METHIONINE	0.32	%
METH+CYS	0.59	%
LYSINE	0.80	%
TRYPTOPHAN	0.19	%
LINOLEIC ACID	1.46	%
DRY MATTER	87.95	%
XANTHOPHYLL	20.75	MG/KG

REFERENCES

Anderson, D. L. 1964. Effect of body size and dietary energy on the protein requirement of turkey breeders. Poultry Sci. 43:59-64.

Anderson, J. O., R. K. Dalai and R. E. Warnick 1973. Value of several sulfur-containing compounds in chick and poult diets. Poultry Sci. 52:1994-1995.

Atkinson, R. L., J. W. Bradley and J. R. Couch 1974. Effect of adding lysine and methionine to turkey breeder rations. Poultry Sci. 53:1632.

Atkinson, R. L., A. A. Kurnick, T. M. Ferguson, B. L. Reid, J. M. Quisenberry and J. R. Couch. 1957. Protein and energy levels for turkey starting diets. Poultry Sci. 36:767-773.

Aukland, J. N. 1973. Relationships between body weight and bone length at one day and at six weeks of age in male turkeys fed on adequate and low protein starter diets. Brit. Poultry Sci. 14:205-208.

Aukland, J.N., and T. R. Morris 1971. The effect of dietary nutrient concentration and calorie to protein ratio on growth and body composition of male and female turkey poults. Brit. Poultry Sci. 12:305-311.

Baldini, J. T., J. P. Marvel and H. R. Rosenberg 1957. The effect of the productive energy level of the diet on the methionine requirement of the poult. Poultry Sci. 36:1031-1035.

Balloun, S. L., and R. E. Phillips 1957. Lysine and protein requirements of Bronze turkeys. Poultry Sci. 36:884-891.

Balloun, S. L., W. J. Owings, J. L. Sell and R. E. Phillips 1959. Energy and protein requirements for turkey starting diets. Poultry Sci. 38:1328-1340.

Bird, F. H. 1950. The tryptophan requirement of turkey poults. Poultry Sci. 29:737-740.

Blair, M. E., L. M. Potter, B. A. Bliss, and J. R. Shelton 1986. Methionine, choline and sulfate supplementation of practical-type diets for young turkeys. Poultry Sci. 65: 130-137.

Day, E. J., and J. E. Hill 1957. The effect of calorie-protein ratio of the ration on growth and feed efficiency of turkeys. Poultry Sci. 36:773-779.

D'Mello, J.P.F. 1975. Amino acid requirements of the young turkey. Leucine, isoleucine and valine. Brit. Poultry Sci. 16:607-615.

Donaldson, W. E., G. F. Combs and G. L. Romoser 1958. Studies on energy levels in poultry rations. 3. Effect of calorie-protein ratio of the ration on growth, nutrient utilization and body composition of poults. Poultry Sci. 37:614-619.

Dunkelgod, K. E., and R. H. Thayer 1961. Effect of dietary energy on the protein requirements of growing turkeys. Poultry Sci. 40:1068-1079.

Ferguson, T. M., H. P. Vaught, L. D. Matterson, B. L. Reid and

Ferguson, T. M.,H. P. Vaught, L. D. Matterson, B. L. Reid and J. R. Couch. 1957. The effect of different levels of productive energy, protein and methionine upon growth of Broad Breasted Bronze turkey poults. Poultry Sci. 36:124-128.

Ferket, P.R. and E.T. Moran, Jr. 1985 Effect of plane of nutrition from starting through the breeder period on the reproductive performance of tom turkeys. Poultry Sci. 64:2110-2118.

Ferket, P.R., and E.T. Moran, Jr. 1986. Effect of plane of nutrition from starting to and through the breeder period on reproductive performance of hen turkeys. Poultry Sci. 65:1581-1590.

Fritz, J.C., J.H. Hooper, J.L. Halpin and H.P. Moore 1946. Failure of feather pigmentation in bronze poults due to lysine deficiency. J. Nutrition 31:387-396.

German, H.L., B.S. Schweigert, R.M. Sherwood and L.E. James 1949. Further evidence of the role of lysine in the formation of normal bronze turkey feathers. Poultry Sci. 28:165-167.

Grau, C.R., F.H. Kratzer and V.S. Asmundson 1946. The lysine requirements of poults and chicks. Poultry Sci. 25:529-530.

Harms, R.H., R.E. Buresh and H.R. Wilson 1984. The influence of the grower diet and the fat in the layer diet on performance of turkey hens. Poultry Sci. 63:1634-1637.

Hurwitz, S., I. Ben-Gal, I. Bartov and H. Talpaz 1983. The response of growing turkeys to dietary nutrient density. Poultry Sci. 62:875-881.

Jackson, S., and L.M. Potter 1984. Influence of basic and branched chain amino acids on the lysine and valine requirements of young turkeys. Poultry Sci. 63:2391-2398.

Jackson, C. D., R. H. Thayer, G. G. Walker, M. L. Burrus, R. D Morrison, E. C. Nelson and A. L. Malle 1974. Protein and energy intake requirements of caged turkey breeder hens. Poultry Sci. 53: 1940

Jensen, L. S. 1974. Efficiency of utilization of lipid versus non-lipid metabolizable calories by growing turkeys. World's Poultry Congress Proc. XV: 363-365.

Jensen, L. S., and L. Falen. 1973. Effect of pelleting on the "extra caloric" effect of dietary fat for developing turkeys. Poultry Sci. 52:2342-2344.

Jensen, L. S., G. W. Schumaier and J. D. Latshaw 1970. "Extra caloric" effect of dietary fat for developing turkeys as influenced by calorie-protein ratio. Poultry Sci. 49:1697-1704.

Jowsey, J. R., R. M. Blakely and H. I. Macgregor 1958. Feeding for early marketing of turkey roasters under Canadian requirements for fat. Poultry Sci. 37: 1216.

Kratzer, F. H., F. H. Bird, V. S. Asmundson and S. Lepkovsky 1947. The arginine requirement of young turkey poults. J. Nutrition 34: 167-171.

Kratzer, F. H., P. N. Davis and B. J. Marshall 1956. The protein and lysine requirements of turkeys at various ages. Poultry Sci. 35:197-202.

Kratzer, F. H., and P. Vohra 1956. Effect of dietary lysine on tyrosinase activity in feather pulp of turkey poults. Fed. Proc. 15:559-560.

Kratzer, F. H., and D. E. Williams 1949. The relation of lysine in the diet to the develoment of feather pigment in turkey poults. Poultry Sci. 28:772.

Kratzer, F. H., D. E. Williams and B. Marshall 1950. The relation of lysine and protein level in the ration to the development of feather pigment in turkey poults. Poultry Sci. 29:285-292.

Kratzer, F. H., D. E. Williams and B. Marshall 1952. The requirement for isoleucine and the activities of its isomers for the growth of turkey poults. J. Nutrition 47:631-635.

Kuhl, H. J., and T. W. Sullivan 1974. Protein, supplemental methionine and inorganic sulfate levels for starting poults. Poultry Sci. 53:1945.

Leeson, S., K. N. Boorman and D. Lewis 1974. Metabolisable energy studies with turkeys. Metabolisable energy of dietary ingredients. Brit. Poultry Sci. 15:183-190.

Minear, L. R., D. L. Miller and S. L. Balloun 1972. Protein requiremnts of turkey breeder hens. Poultry Sci. 51:2040-2043.

Moran, E. T., Jr., P. R. Ferket and J. R. Blackman 1983. Maintenance nitrogen requirement of the turkey breeder hen with an estimate of associated essential amino acid needs. Poultry Sci. 62: 1823-1829.

Moran, E.T., Jr., P.R. Ferket, R.J. Etches and J.R. Blackman 1983. Influence of a low plane of nutrition during sexual development on subsequent performance of Small White breeder toms. Poultry Sci. 62:1093-1100.

Murillo, M., and L. S. Jensen 1974. Relationship of methionine level to dermatitis in turkey poults. Poultry Sci. 53:1959.

Noll, Sally L., P. E. Waibel, R. D. Cook and J. A. Witmer 1984. Biopotency of methionine sources for young turkeys. Poultry Sci. 63:2458-2470.

Potter, L. M., and J. R. Shelton 1974. Methionine and protein requirements of young turkeys. Poultry Sci. 53:1967-1968.

Rosebrough, R.W., N.C. Steele, J.P. McMurtry, M.P. Richards and C.C. Calvert 1983. Role of protein and energy in the regulation of energy metabolism and reproductive performance of Large White turkey hens. Poultry Sci. 62:2452-2459.

Salmon, R. E. 1984. Effect of grower and finisher protein on performance, carcass grade, and meat yield of turkey broilers. Poultry Sci. 63:1980-1986.

Saxena, H. C., and J. McGinnis 1952. Effect of DL-methionine on feed utilization by chicks and turkey poults. Wash. Agr. Exp. Circ. 197:1-5.

Scott, H.M., and L.F. Payne 1941. The influence of restricted food intake on the reproductive performance of breeding turkeys. Poultry Sci. 20:395-401.

Scott, M. L. 1986. NUTRITION OF HUMANS AND SELECTED ANIMAL SPECIES. John Wiley & Sons, 605 Third Ave. New York

Scott, M. L., G. F. Heuser and L. C. Norris 1948. Energy, protein and unidentified vitamins in poult nutrition. Poultry Sci. 27:773-780.

Scott, M. L., M. C. Nesheim and R. J. Young 1982. NUTRITION OF THE CHICKEN. M. L. Scott & Assoc. Box 816, Ithaca, NY 14850.

Sell, J L., R. J. Hasiak, and W. J. Owings 1985. Independent effects of dietary metabolizable energy and protein concentrations on performance and carcass characteristics of tom turkeys. Poultry Sci. 64:1527-1535.

Sell, J. L., A. Krogdahl, and Nana Hanyu 1986. Influence of age on utilization of supplemental fats by young turkeys. Poultry Sci. 65: 546-554.

Sell, J. L., and W. J. Owings 1984. Influence of feeding supplemental fat by age sequence on the performance of growing turkeys. Poultry Sci. 63: 1184-1189.

Sherman, W. C., G. A. Donovan and W. M. Reynolds 1960. Evaluation of lysine in turkey rations. Poultry Sci. 39:1293.

Siopes, T. D. 1983. Effect of intermittent lighting on energy savings and semen characteristics of breeder tom turkeys. Poultry Sci. 62:2265-2270.

Sloan, D. R., and R. H. Harms 1972. Utilization of inorganic sulfate by turkey poults. Poultry Sci. 51: 1673-1675.

Slinger, S. J., I. R. Sibbald and W. F. Pepper 1964. The relative abilities of two breeds of chickens and two varieties of turkeys to metabolize dietary energy and dietary nitrogen. Poultry Sci. 43:329-333.

Snetsinger, D. C., D. G. Britzman, R. C. Fitzsimmons and P. E. Waibel 1964. The L-phenylalanine and L-valine requirement of the turkey poult and the utilization of their D-isomers. Poultry Sci. 43:675-681.

Snetsinger, D. C., P. E. Waibel and R. C. Fitzsimmons 1962. Studies with crystalline amino acid diets for the turkey poult. Poultry Sci. 41:1429-1433.

Summers, J. D., S. Leeson, M. Bedford and Diane Spratt 1985. Influence of dietary protein and energy on performance and carcass composition of heavy turkeys. Poultry Sci. 64: 1921-1933.

Summers, J. D., and E. T. Moran, Jr. 1971. Protein requirement of poults to 8 weeks of age. Poultry Sci. 50:858-861.

Summers, J. D., W. F. Pepper, E. T. Moran and J. D. McConachie 1968. Protein requirements of fast growing strains of Large White and broiler type turkeys. Poultry Sci. 47:536.

Touchburn, S. P., and E. C. Naber 1966. The energy value of fats for growing turkeys. Proc. 13th World Poultry Cong. 13:190-195.

Touchburn, S. P., and E. C. Naber 1969. Metabolizable energy determinations with growing turkeys. Fed. Proc. 28:306.

Tuttle, W. L., and S. L. Balloun 1974. Lysine requirements of starting and growing turkeys. Poultry Sci. 53:1698-1704.

Vohra, P., and F. H. Kratzer 1959. The effect of phenylalanine deficiency on the growth and feather pigmentation of turkey poults. Poultry Sci. 38:902-906.

Waibel, P. E. 1959. Methionine and lysine in rations for turkey poults under various dietary conditions. Poultry Sci. 38:712-721.

Warnick, R. E., and J. O. Anderson 1973. Essential amino acid levels for starting turkey poults. Poultry Sci. 52:445-452.

Warnick, R. E., and J. O. Anderson 1973a. Overall level of essental amino acids in rations for poults. Poultry Sci. 52: 2099.

Wolford, J. H., R. K. Ringer, T. H. Coleman and H. C. Zindel 1963. Individual feed consumption of turkey breeder hens and the correlation of feed intake, body weight and egg production. Poultry Sci. 42:599-604.

Zaporozhchenko, I. 1974. Effect of different levels of lysine and protein on morphology and incubating quality of eggs. Nutr. Abst. & Revs.

CHAPTER 3

MINERAL REQUIREMENTS OF TURKEYS

Qualitatively, the turkey requires the same thirteen inorganic elements that are required by chickens and most other animals. These are calcium and phosphorus (the structural elements that make up the major part of the skeleton); sodium, potassium and chloride (the electrolytes that control homeostasis); magnesium which has many functions; and the trace elements, iron, copper, manganese, zinc, iodide, selenium and molybdenum. Though fluoride, chromium and several other elements have been reported by some workers to be required by rats, chicks or other animals, no evidence exists to indicate that any of these are needed by turkeys. If needed, ample levels must be present in normal feedstuffs.

The essential inorganic elements and their required levels for starting, growing, finishing and breeding turkeys are shown in Table 3.1.

The quantitative mineral requirements of turkeys differ in many instances from those of chickens and other animals. Therefore, a detailed discussion of each mineral and the factors involved in its utilization by turkeys will be presented.

CALCIUM AND PHOSPHORUS

Early commercial turkey starting rations, prior to 1950, contained calcium levels of about 2% and phosphorus levels of about 1%. These values were based on studies of Mussehl and Ackerson (1935), Hammond, et al. (1944), Fritz, et al. (1945), Evans and Brant (1945), Motzok and Slinger (1948) and other early experiments. During the 1960's it became apparent that these levels were higher than desirable, and were due to poor availability for turkeys of the phosphorus present in several of the phosphorus sources being used.

Further studies of the phosphorus requirements by Blaylock and associates (1961), Pensack and White-Stevens (1961), Formica, et al. (1962), indicated that calcium levels of 0.8-1.2% were adequate together with 0.8% total phosphorus for starting poults. Nelson, Jensen and McGinnis (1961), Jones, et al. (1961), Sullivan (1962), Day and Dilworth (1962), reported that 0.6% calcium and 0.6% total phosphorus are adequate for maximum growth and freedom from leg weakness during the 8 to 24 weeks growth period. Because some improvement in tibia ash was obtained at slightly higher levels, both Sullivan and the Washington State workers recommended 0.7% calcium and 0.7% total phosphorus for this turkey growing period.

TABLE 3.1 The mineral requirements of turkeys

Essential inorganic element	Requirement		
	Starting	Growing	Breeding
	per cent of total diet		
Calcium	1.0	0.8	2.0-2.25
Phosphorus, avail.	0.8	0.55	0.45
Sodium	0.18	0.15	0.15
Chloride	0.15	0.15	0.15
Potassium	0.75	0.60	0.60
	ppm	ppm	ppm
Magnesium	660	660	660
Manganese	75	55	60
Iron (total)	88	65	75
Zinc	75	65	75
Copper	10	10	10
Iodide	0.4	0.4	0.4
Selenium (available)[1]	0.2	0.2	0.2

[1] About 25% of the selenium in vegetable materials and 85% of that in animal materials is unavailable.

Although both calcium and phosphorus are involved in many functions, the major need for these elements is for bone formation. Since the ratio of calcium to phosphorus in bone is approximately 2:1, it is logical that the nutritional requirement for these elements bears a ratio of two parts calcium to one part of _available_ phosphorus.

Wilcox and associates (1955) presented evidence of wide variability in the availability to young poults of the phosphorus in many inorganic sources of phosphorus. Gillis and associates (1957) found, in studies with radioactive phosphorus, that the phosphorus in calcium phytate is almost completely unavailable to young turkey poults. Scott, Butters and Ranit (1962) found very poor utilization by poults of the phosphorus in reagent grade, anhydrous dicalcium phosphate ($CaHPO_4$), a phosphorus supplement known to be highly available to chicks. Addition of commercial soybean meal to the purified poult diet caused an improvement in the availability of the phosphorus from the anhydrous dicalcium phosphate.

A clue to the cause of the poor availability of anhydrous dicalcium phosphate came from the work of Gillis, Edwards and Young (1962) who showed that the dihydrate of dicalcium phosphate ($CaHPO_4 \cdot 2H_2O$) is highly available for poults, equivalent to its availability for chicks. Supplee (1962) reported that poults receiving the dihydrated dicalcium phosphate made excellent gains and were free of leg weakness whereas poults fed the anhydrous dicalcium phosphate began to die by the fifth day and survivors showed severe leg weakness by the twelfth day.

A rachitic poult that had received 0.7% anhydrous dicalcium phoshate is shown in Figure 3.1. Also shown in Figure 3.1 is a representative poult with normal tibial calcification on the same diet in which hydrated dicalcium phosphate had been substituted for the anhydrous dicalcium phosphate at a level of only 0.4%.

Griffith and Young (1964) studied fractions of soybean meal in an effort to discover the factor responsible for the benificial effect of soybean meal noted by Scott, Butters and Ranit. Surprisingly, the insoluble hull fraction of the soybean caused the greatest improvement in phosphorus availability. In further studies, Griffith, Young and Scott (1966) showed that the factor was destroyed by treatment of soybean flakes with acid or alkali.

The apparent cause of the poor availability of anhydrous dicalcium phosphate (and very likely many other phosphorus sources) is due to the poor gastric acidity of the proventriculus of the baby poults such that they are unable to dissolve the anhydrous form, but can readily dissolve the hydrated dicalcium phosphate. Ranit (1957) showed the phosphorus in commercial grade dicalcium phosphate, defluorinated phosphate and bone meal to have availabilities similar to those for chicks, but the phosphorus of

Figure 3.1 Almost complete failure of tibial calcification in a poult (left) that received a diet containing anhydrous dicalcium phosphate as the source of phosphorus. The poult at the right, with an intake of only 0.4% phosphorus from hydrated dicalcium phosphate, had normal calcification.

colloidal phosphate and Curacao Island phosphate, like anhydrous dicalcium phosphate, to have very poor availability. Fibrous feedstuffs, such as soybean hulls, may act to increase the acid production in the proventriculus of the poults thereby improving somewhat the availability of the phosphorus from these materials. However it appears desirable, when possible, to avoid the use of these phosphorus supplements for turkey poults.

Waibel and associates undertook an extensive study of phosphorus availability in turkeys, using 47 commercial phosphorus supplements obtained directly from feed manufacturers. Bioassays were run with young poults, using bone ash as the criterion of measurement. One reference source of mono/dicalcium phosphate, known to be of high bio-availability, was assigned an arbitrary value of 100 and was used as the standard for the comparisons. Seven other mono/dicalcium phosphates, 20 dicalcium phosphates, and 20 defluorinated phosphates were compared to this standard. The availabilities of the mono/dicalcium, the dicalcium, and the defluorinated phosphates, compared to the standard, were 93.6 $\pm$ 7.6; 88.3 $\pm$ 8.2; and 70.2 $\pm$ 7.2, respectively. Averaging the results with each type of supplement, the total phosphorus requirements of the poults were found to be 0.74, 0.76, and 0.83% of the diet, respectively, with the mono/dicalcium, the dicalcium or the defluorinated phoshates. The available phosphorus allowance for starting poults of 0.8%, given in Table 3.1, represents a good margin of safety over minimum requirements without being excessive.

In an independent study, Potchanakorn and Potter (1987) used hydrated dicalcium phosphate as the standard to which they compared the availabilities of the phosphorus in 13 different sources in young turkey poults. Compared to the excellent availability of the phosphorus in the hydrated dicalcium phosphate (set arbitrarily at 100), the availability of the phosphorus in three samples, each, of commercial monocalcium phosphates (21% P) and commercial dicalcium phosphates (18.5% P) were found to be 93 and 81, respectively. Defluorinated phosphates were found to average about 75% the availability of the standard hydrated dicalcium phosphate. These studies, in confirmation of the work of Waibel et al.(described above), indicate a need to increase the phosphorus level of the diet by approximately 0.4% when defluorinated phosphates are used as the major phosphorus supplement, in comparison with the use of commercial dicalcium phosphates.

It is quite likely that the ratio of 1% calcium to 0.8% "available" phosphorus shown in Table 3.1 as the requirements for starting poults actually represents, in many instances, a ratio of 2 parts calcium to one part of _truly available_ phosphorus for the turkey poult.

Although the findings given above are very helpful, until the truly available phosphorus content of all poultry feedstuffs has been studied thoroughly with turkeys, it is necessary to use the phosphorus-availability values for the chicken, such as those given in the textbook, "Nutrition of the Chicken" by Scott, Nesheim and Young. The phosphorus requirements given in Table 3.1 are based upon studies using the availability values determined with the chickens referred to above.

CALCIUM AND PHOSPHORUS FOR BREEDERS

The calcium requirements of breeding turkeys are considerably lower, as percentages of the diet, than those of chickens. This is due largely to the much greater feed intake of turkey hens compared to that of laying chickens.

The early studies of Jensen and associates (1963,1964) appear to have established the calcium requirement of turkey breeders. In low-energy breeding diets as little as 1.75% calcium was sufficient. With higher-energy diets the optimum level af calcium was 2.25%. These results have been confirmed by numerous others (Atkinson, et al.,1964; Balloun and Miller, 1964; Arends and associates, 1967; Nestor, et al., 1972). All of these studies were well confirmed and summarized by Waldroup and associates who reported that caged turkey breeder hens needed no more than 2.25% calcium and 0.3% available phosphorus for maximum production, fertility, hatchability and egg shell quality.

Calculation of the calcium requirement

A laying chicken producing a 65-gram egg requires about 3.7 grams of calcium intake per day which can be obtained by the consumption of 100 grams of a feed containing 3.7% calcium. The breeding turkey hen consumes about 250-300 grams of feed per day. The 2.25% calcium level given as the calcium requirement in Table 3.1 is sufficient such that with a feed intake of 250 grams, the hen will receive 5.6 grams of calcium per day; with a 300 gram feed intake, the diet need contain only 2% calcium to assure a calcium intake of 6 grams.

Calcium intakes of 5.6-6.0 grams per day are sufficient for good egg shell development even though the turkey egg is considerably larger than that of the chicken.

The feeding of diets formulated for breeding chickens, or any other diets containing 3.5-4.0% calcium, to turkey breeding hens is very likely to lead to serious problems due to the excessive intake of calcium. This fact was brought to the attention of the author in the 1960's when he was called to a large turkey breeding ranch in California to try to determine the cause of a precipitous drop in hatchability. It was thought that the problem could not possibly be due to nutrition because the same feed was producing very good results on several other turkey breeding ranches.

It was the month of February. Eight thousand breeding turkeys were housed in a new facility on the slope of Mount Palomar. There were patches of snow nearby. The outside temperature was in the 30's F. Upon entering the breeder house, it was noted that all of the turkeys were at the feeders eating, and that they continued to eat all of the time we were there to observe them. Questioning brought out the fact that because most of the breeding turkeys in California were located near the desert where the environmental temperature is usually quite warm, the metabolizable energy content of the breeder diet had been set at about 1150 kcal. per pound and the calcium had been increased to 3.3%. Inspection of some of the embryos that had died disclosed abnormalities such as poorly formed or absence of legs, indicative of a zinc deficiency (Kienholz, et al., 1961). Apparently the high feed intake of a high-calcium diet was causing occlusion and loss of zinc from the intestines, even though a supposedly adequate level of zinc was present in the diet.

When the calcium level of the diet was reduced to 2.25% and the metabolizable energy increased to 1250 kcal/lb, and additional zinc was added to the breeder diet, hatchability soon returned from the low of 30% to its original 80% of total eggs.

Phosphorus for breeders

Most of the studies of phosphorus with turkey breeders indicate the requirement to be no greater than 0.3% available phosphorus. However, in view of the variations in availability of phosphorus from various feedstuffs for turkeys, the recommended level of available phosphorus for breeding turkeys is set at 0.45% in Table 3.1.

SODIUM, POTASSIUM AND CHLORIDE

Sodium and chloride, along with potassium, phosphates, bicarbonates and proteins, function to maintain homeostasis, such as normal osmotic relationships, and optimal pH (electolyte balance) throughout the animal body.

The sodium and chloride requirements of turkeys given in Table 3.1 are only slightly different from those of chickens. The osmotic density of turkey plasma, like that of chickens, is equivalent to a 1 % sodium chloride solution, a somewhat higher osmotic level than the plasma of humans and most mammals which is equivalent to a 0.9 % sodium chloride solution.

Sodium

Kumpost and Sullivan (1966) reported that the sodium requirement of poults, for maximum growth and efficiency of feed utilization, ranged from 0.15 to 0.20% of the diet. Harms (1982) pin-pointed the sodium requirement at 0.14% added to a diet containing 0.04%, or a total sodium requirement of 0.18%.

Harms, Buresh and Wilson (1985) conducted two experiments to determine the sodium requirement of Large White turkey breeding hens. Egg production of the turkey hens receiving the sodium-free basal diet dropped to zero within 70 days. The total sodium requirement for maximum production, in turkey hens receiving a corn-soya practical diet was 0.1 %. The NRC (1984) recommended sodium level of 0.15%, therefore apparently represents a 50% margin over the minimum requirement of turkey breeding hens.

Chloride

Harms (1982) reported the chloride requirement to be 0.126% of the diet in the presence of adequate sodium. This level is somewhat in accord with the findings of Kubichek and Sullivan (1973) who had found the chloride requirement of poults to be more than 0.125% but less than 0.145%.

In Large White turkey breeders, the basal chloride levels of 0.03% in the diet and 20 ppm in the drinking water were sufficient for maximum egg production, fertility and hatchability. It was necessary to supplement the diet with 0.09% chloride for maximum shell quality as measured by specific gravity of the eggs. Thus the minimum total chloride requirement of turkey breeding hens is no more than 0.13%.

Symptoms of Deficiency

Symptoms of sodium deficiency are extreme weakness, softening of the bones, gonadal inactivity, adrenal hypertrophy and changes in cellular functions. There is a decreased feed consumption and a decreased blood fluid volume. This is accompanied by a drop in blood pressure and decreased adrenal function leading to a rise in blood uric acid. If not corrected the syndrome ends in death. Pang, et al. (1978) described the dehydration and all of the symptoms that accompany it in sodium-deficient poults.

In adult turkeys, egg production decreases and, in some cases, cannibalism occurs.

Harms et al. (1982,1983) showed that a deficiency of chloride also causes very poor growth and poor efficiency of feed utilization in young poults. Kubichek and Sullivan reported that chloride-deficient poults exhibited extremely poor growth, high mortality, dehydration and nervous symptoms similar to those described by Leach and Nesheim (1963) for chloride-deficient chicks. Excitement caused the poults to fall forward, extending their legs to the rear with their wings outstreched. For some, these tetanic seizures lasted only 2-3 minutes, for others they ended in death.

Effects of excess salt

Matterson, Scott and Jungherr (1946) investigated the possiblity, proposed by others, that edema and ascites in turkeys may be due to intakes of slight excesses of salt in the diet or drinking water. Their results indicated that poults readily tolerate levels of sodium chloride up to 2% in the diet. Atkinson et al. (1954) reported that carcasses of turkeys fed 2% salt in the starter diet were significantly heavier and contained significantly more moisture than those fed a normal salt level. The weight difference was due entirely to moisture, since the carcass weights on a dry basis were equivalent.

Krista, Carlson and Olson (1961) reported that a level of 4000 ppm of sodium chloride in drinking water caused poor growth and mortality in young poults. Jelinkova, Vesely and Dvorak (1964) indicated that quite high levels of dietary salt are not toxic as long as the turkeys have plenty of pure, salt-free water to drink and are consuming a nutritionally-balanced diet. However, Pang, et al. (1979) described the work of others implicating saline waters with ascites in turkeys and observed that even hypotonic levels of salt in the drinking water produced edema and ascites when given during the period from 5 to 9 days of age. They postulated that a renal insufficiency at this age may be responsible for this susceptibility to the toxic effects of saline waters.

Potassium

Potassium is present in the animal body mainly inside the cells where it carries out many of the same functions of homeostasis that are performed by sodium in the blood plasma and interstitial fluids.

While numerous studies indicate that the potassium requirement of chicks is no greater than 0.4%, Supplee and associates at the University of Maryland found the young poult to require at least 0.6% dietary potassium. The NRC has set the requirement of the young, starting poult at 0.7% of the diet.

This is significant in view of the part that potassium plays in cases of stress, which appears to be especially important in turkey production.

Turkeys are exposed to many stresses during their long growing period. Stress causes the animals to lose potassium. During stress, plasma protein is elevated, causing the kidney, under the influence of adreno-cortical hormone, to discharge potassium into the urine. If the potassium content of the diet is adequate, the animal can regain its lost potassium during its adaptation to the stress. Animals cannot adapt to stress if the diet is deficient in potassium.

Symptoms of deficiency

The main symptoms of potassium deficiency are severe over-all muscle weakness, poor intestinal tone with intestinal distention, cardiac weakness and weakness of the respiratory muscles with their ultimate failure resulting in death.

Chavez and Kratzer (1973,1973a,1974) studied the effect of potassium deficiency on growth, food intake and bone calcification in turkey poults. The potassium requirement for maximum growth, best efficiency of feed utilization and minimum mortality was 0.6-0.75% of the diet. Increasing the potassium to 1.25% appeared to be toxic, causing some mortality and a significant decrease in growth rate. Bone growth was completely arrested in poults fed a potassium-free diet for one week, indicating an important role of potassium in bone calcification. In view of these findings, it appears desirable to set the potassium requirement of starting poults at 0.75%, and to be sure that the grower, finisher and breeder diets contain at least 0.6% potassium.

Because soybean meal contains approximately 2% potassium, it usually is not necessary to add potassium to turkey diets based largely on soybean meal as the protein supplement. However, in view of the great importance of potassium for young poults, the nutritionist should calculate the potassium level in the diet formulations and make sure of an adequate level of potassium.

MAGNESIUM, IRON AND COPPER

The magnesium, iron and copper requirements of turkeys apparently do not differ from those of chickens.

Magnesium

Keene (1963) and Sullivan (1964) studied the magnesium requirements of starting poults. Keene reported the minimum magnesium requirement to be 410 ppm for maximum results. Diets containing as much as 1800 ppm of magnesium showed no evidence of toxicity. Sullivan indicated that the magnesium requirement of starting poults was greater than 365 ppm but no higher than 465 ppm, thus in fairly good agreement with Keene. Sullivan found that practical, commercial rations for turkeys did not require magnesium supplementation.

Symptoms of magnesium deficiency in poults are similar to those in chicks and other animals and include poor growth, gasping, nervous tremors, convulsions, coma and death.

Iron

Iron is required by all animals for hemoglobin formation. A deficiency, therefore results in a normocytic, hypochromic anemia. About 60% of the total body iron is present in the blood hemoglobin; about 7% in the myoglobin. The remainder is stored in ferritin and hemosiderin. Small amounts are present in iron-containing enzymes, such as the cytochromes.

Although the daily loss of iron, normally, is very small, and therefore the amount that must be absorbed from the intestines is equally small, the dietary requirement for iron is quite large because of poor absorption from the intestines. The presence of heme (largely present in blood) in the diet helps the absorption of iron. Even with diets containing heme, however, iron absorption is increased only from about 3% from a non-heme diet to about 25% in a heme-containing diet.

Al-Ubaidi and Sullivan (1963) found a requirement of 48 ppm of iron for normal growth in starting poults, and a requirement of 58 ppm for maximum hemoglobin formation. Balasch and Planas (1972), of Spain, found that iron is taken up directly from transferrin by the hemoglobin of the reticulocytes. Radioactive iron was found to be released during blood cell destruction. Since the life span of turkey erythrocytes is only about 25 days, there is comparatively rapid turn-over of iron in turkey poults.

Other than anemia, no iron deficiency symptoms have been described for turkeys. However, because iron is needed in many critical enzymes in all of the higher animals, it is likely that symptoms described for other birds and mammals also can occur in turkeys.

Anoxia, due to low hemoglobin, can produce listlessness, poor growth and vascular congestion of the heart, liver, kidneys and other organs of the body. Severe iron deficiency in New Hampshire Red chickens was shown by Davis, Norris and Kratzer (1968) to bring about complete depigmentation of the feathers. A similar phenomenon may occur in Bronze turkeys receiving diets very deficient in iron.

Copper

Copper not only is needed together with iron for normal hemoglobin formation, but also as a component of many very important enzymes in all animals. Among these are cytochrome-c oxidase, superoxide dismutase and many other oxidases. One important oxidase (lysyl oxidase) is involved in the formation of desmosines an essential part of elastin, such as that present in the wall of the aorta. Thus, a severe deficiency of copper could lead to aortic rupture. Although turkeys often suffer aortic ruptures, there is no evidence thus far to implicate copper deficiency in this disorder of turkeys reared under commercial conditions.

Evans and Wiederanders (1967) determined total plasma copper, indirect-reacting copper, erythrocyte copper and ceruloplasmin oxidase activities in eight different species. Total plasma copper was lowest in turkeys and peacocks. The turkey had the lowest erythrocyte copper as well. No ceruloplasmin activity was found in either the turkey or the peacock. This indicates that turkeys may have a relatively poor storage mechanism for copper.

High dietary levels of copper

Waibel and associates (1964) found a great variation in the tolerance of turkeys to dietary copper levels. In some experiments using a purified diet, dietary copper at only 50 ppm proved highly toxic, whereas poults receiving a natural diet performed well and continued to do so receiving copper levels up to 800 ppm. Scott and Peter (1965) found that 50 ppm of copper as copper sulfate produced a growth response similar to that obtained with several antibiotics, and no additional growth response occured when this level of copper was added to the diet in combination with the antibiotics.

Aldinger (1966) reported on several experiments in which growth and feed efficiency were improved by use of high levels of copper in the diet of turkey poults.

Peterson and Jensen (1972) found that the toxicity for turkey poults of 900 ppm of silver, as silver acetate, could be overcome by the simultaneous addition to the diet of copper and selenium. The initial finding that dried distiller's solubles counteracted this silver toxicity could now be explained on the basis of the copper content of the distiller's solubles.

In view of the conflicting reports of both beneficial and detrimental effects of high levels of copper, Vohra and Kratzer (1968) set about to determine the outright toxic level in practical turkey rations. This was found to be 676 ppm. Obviously, until a better understanding is at hand regarding the reasons for the variabilities in toxicities, great care should be exercised in the use of high dietary copper levels in practical turkey rations.

MANGANESE

Manganese is required by turkeys, and a deficiency will cause poor growth and "hock disorders". The role of manganese has been relegated to secondary importance because a deficiency usually does not produce typical perosis, which is produced by a deficiency of choline in poults.

Soon after the discovery that manganese was the primary factor responsible for the severe crippling disease of chickens, known as "perosis" or "slipped tendon disease", Mussehl and Ackerson (1939) of the University of Nebraska, and Ringrose, Martin and Insko (1939) of the University of Kentucky initiated studies of manganese deficiency in turkey poults. Using a basal diet very low in manganese, Ringrose et al. reported a high incidence of "perosis" and very poor growth. Mussehl and Ackerson used a poult diet containing a basal level of about 35 ppm manganese and obtained no improvement in growth or any other criterion by the addition of up to 350 ppm of manganese to this diet. They also obtained no evidence of toxicity from the addition of this level of manganese.

Kealy and Sullivan (1966) found that the poult requirement for manganese for maximum growth and freedom from "hock disorders" was influenced by the type of diet used, and ranged from 24 to 72 ppm in diets designed to be adequate in all other nutrients, including ample choline. Evans and associates (1942) emphasized the fact that high dietary levels of calcium and phosphorus greatly increase the manganese requirement and the incidence of "perosis" in manganese-low diets.

Atkinson and associates (1967) reported that the dietary manganese requirement of breeding turkeys for maximum reproductive performance and minimum embryonic mortality was between 54 and 108 ppm, levels much higher than the NRC recommended allowance. It is quite apparent that this requirement needs to be pinpointed more precisely.

Fortunately, the toxic level of manganese far exceeds any possible nutritional level. The minimum toxic level of manganese for turkey poults was found by Vohra and Kratzer (1968) to be 4800 ppm. An antagonistic effect of zinc and copper on the storage of manganese in the liver of poults was reported by Vohra and Heil (1969).

Although early investigators of manganese deficiency in poults reported the occurence of "perosis", no reports of slipped tendon due to manganese deficiency in poults have appeared in the recent studies of the deficiency. Manganese deficient poults do show an enlargement of the hock joint, but may not suffer "perosis" as originally defined. A more detailed discussion of leg weaknesses of turkeys will be presented in Chapter 6.

ZINC

During the late 1950's zinc was discovered to be one of the most important factors required for prevention of severe leg weakness in turkeys. Kratzer and associates (1958) found that poults receiving a purified diet containing isolated soybean protein developed severe hock enlargements. Addition of zinc to the diet improved growth and markedly reduced the incidence and severity of the hock disorder. Approximately 40 ppm of zinc, in addition to the 26 ppm already present in the basal diet, was needed for optimum growth and maximum prevention of the leg weakness. Sullivan (1961) found that 70 ppm of dietary zinc was necessary for growth and most rapid bone and feather development. He reported that the zinc in zinc carbonate and in $ZnSO4.7H2_O$ was more available than that in zinc oxide.

Vohra and Kratzer (1966) showed that addition of ethylene diamine tetra-acetic acid (EDTA) to the diet prevented much of the binding of zinc by the natural phytic acid in the diet, thereby rendering the zinc much more available for absorption by the poults. They reported the toxic level of zinc for poults to be approximately 4000 ppm. Even this toxicity could be overcome by adding EDTA to the diet.

SELENIUM

Selenium nutrition is intimately associated with vitamin E nutrition. The earliest report of a syndrome of turkey poults now known to be due largely to selemium deficiency, was gizzard myopathy. At that time, Jungherr and Pappenheimer (1937) thought the disease to be due simply to vitamin E deficiency.

Following the discovery of the nutritional need for selenium for prevention of necrotic liver degeneration in rats (Schwarz and Foltz, 1957) and exudative diathesis in chicks (Scott, et al., 1957), studies were undertaken in several laboratories to determine the effects of selenium deficiency in poults.

Creech et al. (1957) and Ferguson et al. (1964) reported that, although not major signs of vitamin E deficiency in poults, both exudative diathesis and nutritional muscular dystrophy (ofthe skeletal muscles) do occur in poults fed very deficient diets. In 1963, Walter and Jensen reported selenium to be effective in preventing this muscular dystrophy but, unlike chick muscular dystrophy, the skeletal muscular dystrophy of poults is not prevented by high levels of the sulfur-containing amino acids.

The selenium-responsive disease of poults was brought sharply to the attention of the author in 1964 when several commercial flocks of poults in Ohio were found to grow poorly and suffer high mortality with no overt signs of disease except for a severe hyaline degeneration of the gizzard muscle. Upon investigation, it was found that both the corn and soybean meal used in the commercial diets was produced locally in Ohio and Indiana, on soils shown by Muth and Allaway to be very low in selenium and to produce grains and forages so low in selenium that they failed to prevent "white muscle disease" in lambs and calves.

Poults showing myopathy of the gizzard were found in four flocks, totalling about 15,000 turkeys. The feed company nutritionist described the outbreak as follows: "All poults were from a late hatch, from a breeding flock located in northern Indiana. Histological examinations by Dr. Frank Mitchell (a veterinarian) revealed extensive acute coagulation necrosis and fibrous tissue replacement involving musculature of the gizzard. Mitchell observed that he had not previously encountered cases similar to this in turkeys, but coagulation necrosis of muscle fibers is a principal pathologic feature in vitamin E-deficient sheep, cattle and other species. Similar pathology also was observed in the myocardium of poults from one of the flocks".

Immediately following this severe outbreak, experiments were undertaken at Cornell (Scott, et al., 1967) to investigate the effects of vitamin E and selenium in turkeys under conditions similar to those which had prevailed in the commercial flocks in Ohio. Both the corn and soybean meal used in this investigation were samples from the same area of Ohio in which the problem had occurred. A purified diet, designed to be very low in vitamin E and selenium, also was used in the experiment.

Severe myopathies of both the gizzard and heart were obtained in poults receiving either the commercial-type or the purified diets. Photographs of some affected gizzards are shown in Figure 3.2. Photomicrographs of the gizzards (Figure 3.3) presented the same picture described above by Dr. Mitchell. Degeneration of the heart muscle was so severe that blood leaked out of the heart into the pericardium (Figure 3.4).

Additions of vitamin E and methionine to the practical diet improved growth, but the myopathies were not prevented until this diet was supplemented with at least 0.1 ppm selenium as sodium selenite. The selenium requirement in the practical diet depended somewhat upon the amount of vitamin E present in the diet. It ranged from approximately 0.18 ppm Se in the presence of added vitamin E to 0.28 ppm Se in the absence of supplemental vitamin E.

Symptoms of selenium deficiency in young poults are: 1) myopathy of the smooth (gizzard) muscle; 2) myopathy of the cardiac (heart) muscle; 3) and myopathy of the skeletal muscle. Selenium appears to be the primary nutritional factor required for prevention of these diseases. Vitamin E apparently has little or no effect in the absence of selenium, but can reduce the amount of selenium needed to prevent these disorders. Sulfur amino acids

Figure 3.2 Severe myopathy of the gizzard of a selenium-deficient poult (left). Normal gizzard musculature is shown at the right.

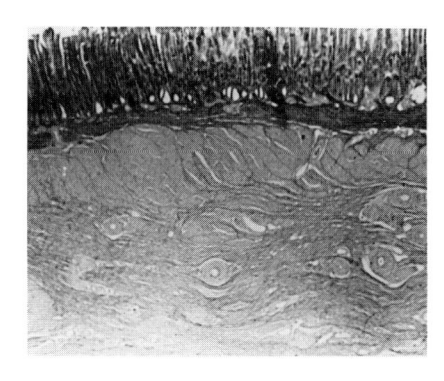

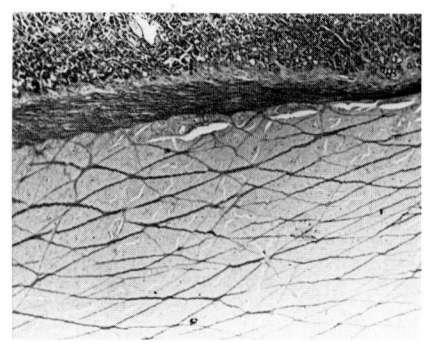

Figure 3.3 Photomicrographs of the selenium-deficient turkey gizzard (left). Normal gizzard cells are shown at the right.

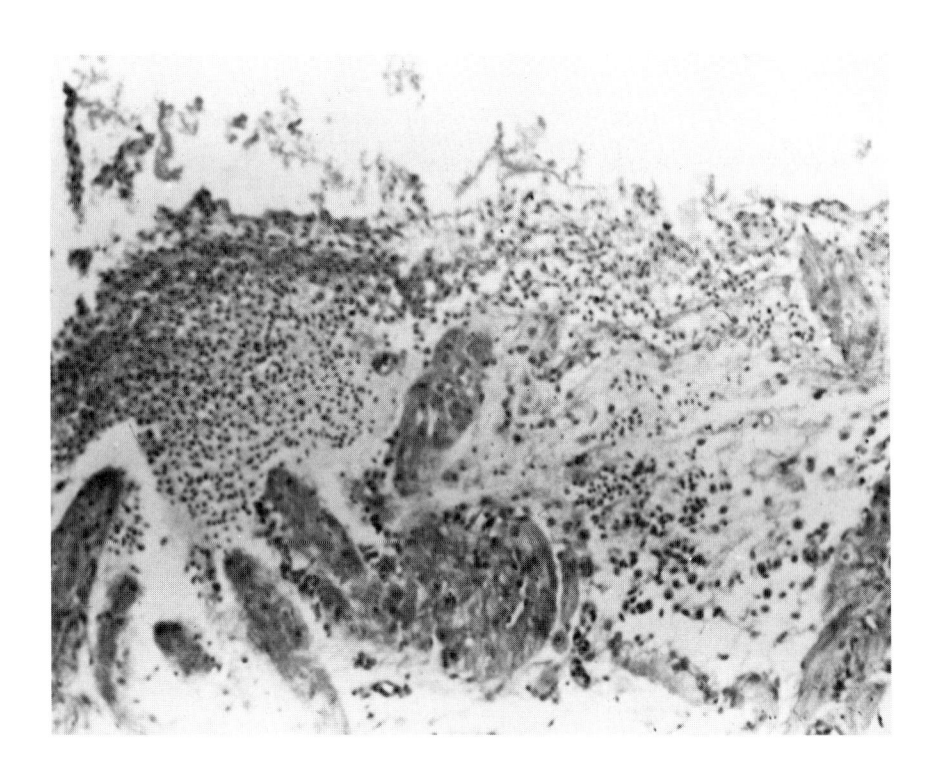

Figure 3.4 Photomicrograph of the heart muscle of a selenium-deficient poult. Note the flow of blood cells out of the heart into the pericardium in the upper part of the slide.

are completely ineffective in the prevention of these myopathies (Walter and Jensen,1963; Scott and associates, 1967).

Studies on the effects of using dietary levels of selenium somewhat in excess of requirements

Scott, et al. (1967) found no deleterious effects from addition of 0.4 ppm Se to a practical diet from a high selenium area of the United States, which contained 0.6 ppm Se from natural sources. Cantor and Scott 1972), in intensive studies showed that dietary supplementation with selenium, up to levels of 1.0 ppm, did not increase blood or tissue levels appreciably above those present with minimum nutritional levels of selenium supplementation. These results were further confirmed by Cantor and associates (1982), who showed that addition of selenium, either as sodium selenate or as selenomethionine, caused marked improvements in growth, and efficiency of feed utilization, prevented gizzard myopathy and reduced the level of plasma glutamic-oxaloacetic transaminase (PGOT) in poults without causing any accumulation of selenium in the blood or tissues. Good increases in both plasma selenium and Se-dependent glutathione peroxidase occured with the increasing levels of dietary selenium.

Selenium toxicity

Selenium levels of 10-20 ppm or more are toxic for chicks and all animals. Indeed, rats show toxic signs with the continuous feeding of 3-5 ppm of selenium as sodium selenite. High selenium levels in diets of breeding birds or mammals may produce a high incidence of teratogeny in the progeny. No studies of selenium toxicity appear to have been conducted with turkeys. Quite likely, the levels found to be toxic for chicks and other animals would be toxic for turkeys.

IODINE

The iodine requirement of turkeys for optimum thyroid function has been set at 0.4 ppm by the NRC (1984). Since little, if any, experimental work has been conducted on this requirement, it appears that the recommendation for poults is based upon the requirement of chicks with a small increase as a margin of safety. This appears plausible, since use of this level in practice apparently is sufficient.

MOLYBDENUM

Richert and Westerfeld (1953) showed molybdenum to be an important part of the enzyme, xanthine oxidase. This is a very important enzyme in all animals, but especially important in chickens and turkeys because of the need of these species to excrete all of the nitrogen products of protein metabolism as uric acid.

Xanthine oxidase is needed for the formation of uric acid from these lower nitrogenous products. Reid et al. (1957) obtained a growth response in poults upon the addition of 0.0254 ppm molybdenum to a purified basal diet.

The NRC (1984) does not indicate a recommended dietary level of molybdenum. Undoubtedly, the molybdenum content of natural feedstuffs provides more than enough of this nutrient for all needs.

Because of the well-known interrelationship between high levels of molybdenum and the copper requirement, Kratzer (1952) studied the effects in chicks and poults of the addition of 300 ppm molybdenum to the diets with and without the addition of extra copper. Growth of both the chicks and the poults was depressed about 25% by this high level of molybdenum, and the copper addition had only a slight beneficial effect upon this depression.

Paine (unpublished communication) encountered a condition in broiler chickens in Australia receiving high dietary levels of copper, which he characterized as a "scabby hip syndrome" and which he stated could be prevented by addition of molybdenum and riboflavin to the diet. This has not been confirmed in chickens and never reported in turkeys.

SUMMARY OF MINERAL REQUIREMENTS

Of the thirteen inorganic elements shown above to be required by turkeys, only eight usually require attention in the formulation of most turkey diets under commercial conditions. These are calcium, phosphorus, sodium, chloride, manganese, zinc, iodine and selenium. Of these, chloride is always present in adequate amounts when the diet contains enough sodium and, therefore, requires no special attention. All other minerals are usually present in adequate amounts in the normal feedstuffs used to provide the energy and protein requirements of the diet.

As indicated above, potassium may require attention in certain diets, especially those containing little soybean meal, the best common feedstuff source of potassium. Additional iron may be needed in diets containing no animal products as a source of the heme normally needed to enhance the absorption of iron.

REFERENCES

Aldinger, S. M. 1966. The effect of high copper levels on turkey performance. Poultry Sci. 45: 1065-1066.

Al-Ubaidi, Y. Y., and T. W. Sullivan 1963. Studies on the requirements and interaction of copper and iron in Broad Breasted Bronze turkeys to 4 weeks of age. Poultry Sci. 42: 718-725.

Arends, L. G., D. L. Miller awnd S. L. Balloun 1967. Calcium requirements of the turkey breeder hen. Poultry Sci. 46: 727-730.

Askoy, A. and T. W. Sullivan 1977. Interrelationship of dietary vitamin D3 with potassium, sodium and magnesium in young turkeys. Poultry Sci. 56: 482-491.

Atkinson, R. L., R. V. Boucher and E. W. Callenbach 1954. Weight and moisture content of carcasses of poults fed added sodium chloride. Poultry Sci. 43: 1301.

Atkinson, R. L., J. W. Bradley, J. R. Couch and J. H. Quisenberry 1967. The calcium requirement of breeding turkeys. Poultry Sci. 46: 207-214.

Atkinson, R. L., J. W. Bradley, J. R. Couch and J. H. Quisenberry 1967a Effect of various levels of manganese on the reproductive performance of turkeys. Poultry Sci. 46: 472-475.

Bailey, C. A., S. Linton, R. Brister and C. R. Creger 1986. Effects of graded levels of dietary phosphorus on bone mineralization in the very young poult. Poultry Sci. 65: 1018-1020.

Balasch, J., and J. Planas 1972. Iron metabolism in the duck and turkey. Rev. Espan. Fisiol. 28: 125-128.

Balloun, S. L. And D. L. Miller 1964. Calcium requirements of turkey breeder hens. Poultry Sci. 43: 378-381.

Blaylock, L. G., L. H. Neagle, and C. F. Lefevre 1961. Studies on the calcium and phosphorus requirements of growing turkeys. Poultry Sci. 40: 1381.

Cantor, A. H., P. D. Moorhead and K. I. Brown 1978. Influence of dietary selenium upon reproductive performance in male and female breeder turkeys. Poultry Sci. 57: 1337-1345.

Cantor, A. H., P. D. Moorhead and M. A. Musser 1982. Comparative effects of sodium selenite and selenomethionine upon nutritional muscular dystrophy, selenium-dependent glutathione peroxidase, and tissue selenium concentrations in turkey poults. Poultry Sci. 61: 478-484.

Cantor, A. H., and M. L. Scott 1972. Effect of dietary supplements of sodium selenite on tissue selenium levels in market age turkeys. Poultry Sci. 51: 1790.

Chavez, E., and F. H. Kratzer 1973. The potassium requirement of poults. Poultry Sci. 52: 1542-1544.

Creech, B. G., G. L. Feldman, T. M. Ferguson, B. L. Reid and J. R. Couch. 1957. Exudative diathesis and vitamin E deficiency in turkey poults. J. Nutrition 62: 83-93.

Davis, P. N., L. C. Norris and F. H. Kratzer 1968. Iron utilization and metabolism in the chick. J. Nutrition 94: 407-417.

Day, E. J., and B. C. Dilworth 1962. Dietary phosphorus levels and calcium:phosphorus ratios needed by growing turkeys. Poultry Sci. 41: 1324-1328.

Evans, G. W. and R. E. Wiederanders 1967. Blood copper variation among species. Amer. J. Physiol. 213: 1183-1185.

Evans, R. J. and A. W. Brant 1945. Calcium, phosphorus and vitamin D interrelationships in turkey poult nutrition. Poultry Sci. 24: 404-407.

Evans, R. J., E. I. Robertson, M. Rhian and L. A. Wilhelm 1942. The development of perosis in turkey poults and its prevention. Poultry Sci. 21: 422-429.

Ferguson, T. M., E. M. Omar and J. R. Couch 1964. Muscular dystrophy in avian species. Texas Rep. Biol. Med. 22: 902.

Ferguson, T. M., C. E. Sewell and R. l. Atkinson 1974. Phosphorus levels in the turkey breeder diet. Poultry Sci. 53: 1627-1629.

Formica, S. D., M. J. Smidt, M. M. Bacharach, W. F. Davin and J. C. Fritz. 1962. Calcium and phosphorus requirements of growing turkeys and chickens. Poultry Sci. 41: 771-776.

Foss, J. O. 1941. Salt tolerance of turkey poults. N. D. Agr. Exp. Sta. Bimonthly Bul. 4(1): 7

Gillis, M. B., H. M. Edwards, Jr., and R. J. Young 1962. Studies on the availabilities of calcium orthophosphates to chickens and turkeys. J. Nutrition 78: 155-161.

Gillis, M. B.,K.W. Keane and R. A. Collins 1957. Comparative metabolism of phytate and inorganic P32 by chicks and poults. J. Nutrition 62: 13-26.

Fritz, J. C., J. H. Hooper and H. P. Moore 1945. Calcification in the poult. Poultry Sci. 24: 324-328.

Griffith, M., and R. J. Young 1967. Influence of dietary calcium, vitamin D-3 and fiber on the availability of phosphorus to turkey poults. Poultry Sci. 46: 553-560.

Griffith, M., R. J. Young and M. L. Scott 1966. Influence of soybean meal on growth and phosphorus availability in turkey poults. Poultry Sci. 45: 189-199.

Hammond, J. C., H. E. McClure and W. L. Kellogg 1944. The minimum phosphorus requirements of turkey poults. Poultry Sci. 23: 239-241.

Harms, R. H. 1982. Chloride requirement of young turkeys. Poultry Sci. 61: 2447-2449.

Harms, R. H., R. E. Buresh and H. R. Wilson 1985. Sodium requirement of the turkey hen. Brit. Poultry Sci. 26: 217-220.

Harms, R. H., O. M. Junquiera and H. R. Wilson 1983. Chloride requirement of the turkey breeder hen. Poultry Sci. 62: 2442-2444.

Jelinkova, V., Z. Vesely and J. Dvorak 1964. Water metabolism in turkeys given toxic doses of sodium chloride. Vet. Bul. 34(4): 219.

Jensen, L. S.,H. C. Saxena and J. McGinnis 1963. Nutritional

investigations with turkey hens. 4. Quantitative requirement for calcium. Poultry Sci. 42:604-607.
Jensen, L. S., R. K. Wagstaff, J. McGinnis and F. Parks 1964. Further studies on high calcium diets for turkey hens. Poultry Sci. 43: 1577-1581.
Jones, M. L., C. W. Devoe, R. E. Davies and J. R. Couch 1961. Effect of phosphorus on growth and hock disorder of turkeys 8-23 weeks of age. Poultry Sci. 40: 1419
Jungherr, E. and A. M. Pappenheimer 1937. Nutritional myopathy of the gizzard in turkey. Proc. Soc. Exp. Biol. Med. 37: 520
Kealy, R. D., and T. W. Sullivan 1966. Studies on the manganese requirement and interactions in the diet of young turkeys. Poultry Sci. 45: 1352-1358.
Keene, O. D. 1963. Magnesium requirement of chicks and poults. Diss. Abstr. 24(4): 1317.
Kratzer, F. H. 1952. Effect of dietary molybdenum upon chicks and poults. Proc. Soc. Exp. Biol. Med. 80:483-486.
Kratzer, F. H., and B. Starcher 1963. Quantitative relation of EDTA to availability of zinc for turkey poults. Proc. Soc. Exp. Biol. Med. 113: 424-426.
Kratzer, F. H., P. Vohra, J. B. Allred and P. N. Davis 1958. Effect of zinc upon growth and incidence of perosis in turkey poults. Proc. Soc. Exp. Biol. Med. 98: 205-207.
Krista, L. M., C.W. Carlson and O. E. Olson 1961. Some effects of saline waters on chicks, laying hens, poults and ducklings. Poultry Sci. 40: 938-944.
Kubicek, J. J. and T. W. Sullivan 1973. Dietary chloride requirement of starting turkeys. Poultry Sci. 52: 1903-1909.
Kumpost, H. E. and T. W. Sullivan 1966. Minimum sodium requirement and the interaction of potassium and sodium in the diet of young turkeys Poultry Sci. 45: 1334-1339.
Leach, R. M., Jr., and M. C. Nesheim 1963. Studies on chloride deficiency in chicks. J. Nutrition 81: 193-201.
Matterson, L. D., H. M. Scott and E. Jungherr 1946. Salt tolerance in turkeys. Poultry Sci. 25: 539-540.
Motzok, I., and S. J. Slinger 1948. Studies on the calcium and phosphorus requirement of Broad Breasted Bronze turkeys. Poultry Sci. 27: 486
Mussehl, F. E., and C. W. Ackerson 1939. The effect of adding manganese to a specific ration for growing poults. Poultry Sci. 18: 408.
Neagle, L. H., L. G. Blaylock and J. H. Goihl 1968. Calcium, Phosphorus and vitamin D-3 levels and interactions in turkeys to 4 weeks of age. Poultry Sci. 47:174-180.
Nelson, F. E., L. S. Jensen and J. McGinnis 1961. Requirement of developing turkeys for calcium and phosphorus. Poultry Sci. 40: 407-411.
Nelson, F. E., L. S. Jensen and J. McGinnis 1963. Influences of previous calcium and phosphorus intake and plant phosphorus on the requirement of developing turkeys for calcium and phosphorus. Poultry Sci. 42: 579-585.

Nesheim, M. C., and M. L. Scott 1961. Nutritional effects of selenium compounds in chicks and turkeys. Fed. Proc. 20: 674-678.
Pensack, J. M., and R. H. White-Stevens 1961. The calcium and phosphorus requirements of the turkey poult. Poultry Sci. 40: 1443.
Peterson, R. P., and L. S. Jensen 1972. Interaction of dietary silver with copper and selenium. Poultry Sci. 51: 1849-1850.
Potchanakorn, M., and L. M. Potter 1987. Biological values of phosphorus from various sources for young turkeys. Poultry Sci. 66: 505-513.
Ranit, G. O. 1957. The phosphorus requirement of poults. Philippine Agric. 41: 76-84.
Reid, B. L., A. A. Kurnick, R. N. Burroughs, R. L. Svacha and J. R. Couch 1957. Molybdenum in poult nutrition. Proc. Soc. Exp. Biol. Med. 94: 737-740.
Richert, D. A., and W. W. Westerfeld 1953. Isolation and identification of the xanthine oxidase factor as molybdenum. J. Biol. Chem. 203: 915-923.
Ringrose, A. T., J. H. Martin and W. M. Insko, Jr. 1939. Manganese requirements of turkey poults. Poultry Sci. 18: 409-410.
Schwarz, K., and C. M. Foltz 1957. Selenium as an integral part of factor 3 against dietary necrotic liver degeneration. J. Amer. Chem. Soc. 79: 3292
Scott, M. L., J. G. Bieri, G. M. Briggs, Jr. and K. Schwarz 1957. Prevention of exudative diathesis by factor 3 in chicks on vitamin E-deficient Torula yeast diets. Poultry Sci. 36:1155.
Scott, M. L., H. E. Butters and G. O. Ranit 1962. Studies on the requirements of young poults for available phosphorus. J. Nutrition 78: 223-230.
Scott, M. L., G. Olson, L. Krook and W. R. Brown 1967. Selenium-responsive myopathies of myocardium and of smooth muscle in the young poult. J. Nutrition 91: 573-583.
Scott, M. L., and J. N. Thompson 1971. Selenium content of feedstuffs and effects of dietary selenium levels upon tissue selenium in chicks and poults. Poultry Sci. 50: 1742-1748.
Sewell, C. E., Jr., R. L. Atkinson, J. R. Couch and T. M. Ferguson 1972. The effect of supplemental phosphorus on the reproductive performance of turkey hens and the subsequent effect upon the poults. Poultry Sci. 51: 792-796.
Sullivan, T. M. 1961. The zinc requirement of Broad Breasted Bronze poults. Poultry Sci. 40: 334-340.
Sullivan, T. M. 1962. Studies on the calcium and phosphorus requirements of turkeys 8 to 20 weeks of age. Poultry Sci. 41: 253-259.
Sullivan, T. M. 1964. Studies on the dietary requirement and interaction of magnesium with antibiotics in turkeys to 4 weeks of age. Poultry Sci. 43: 401-405.
Supplee, W. C. 1962. Anhydrous dicalcium phosphate as a source of phosphorus in poult diets. Poultry Sci. 41: 1984-1985.

Supplee, W. C., and G. F. Combs 1959. Studies on the potassium requirement of turkey poults fed purified diets. Poultry Sci. 38: 833-835.
Vohra, P., and J. R. Heil 1969. Dietary interactions between Zn, Mn and Cu for turkey poults. Poultry Sci. 48: 1686.
Vohra, P., and F. H. Kratzer 1968. Zinc, copper and manganese toxicities in turkey poults and their alleviation by EDTA. Poultry Sci. 47: 699-744.
Waibel, P. E., N. A. Nahorniak, H. E. Dziuk, M. M. Walser and W. G. Olson 1984. Bioavailability of phosphorus in commercial phosphate supplements for turkeys. Poultry Sci. 63: 730-737.
Waibel, P. E., D. C. Snetsinger, R. A. BAll and J. H. Sautter 1964. Variation in tolerance of turkeys to dietary copper. Poultry Sci. 43: 504-506.
Waldroup, P. W., J. F. Maxey and L. W. Luther 1974. Studies on the calcium and phosphorus requirements of caged turkey breeder hens. Poultry Sci. 53: 886-888.
Walter, E. D., and L. S. Jensen 1963. Effectiveness of selenium and noneffectiveness of sulfur amino acids in preventimg muscular dystrophy in the turkey poult. J. Nutrition 80: 327-331.
Wilcox R. A., C. W. Carlson, W. Kohlmeyer and G. F. Gastler 1955. The availability of phosphorus from different sources for poults fed practical-type diets. Poultry Sci.

CHAPTER 4

VITAMIN REQUIREMENTS OF TURKEYS

Turkeys have relatively high requirements for all of the vitamins. Turkeys not only need these high levels for normal growth, production and reproduction, but also store high levels of the vitamins in the carcass. Thus turkey meat is one of the richest sources of many of the vitamins.

The vitamin allowances for turkeys are shown in Table 4.1. Because of the critical importance of the vitamins, and because, as will be discussed in detail later, baby turkeys have a poor ability to properly utilize some of the vitamin precursors and pre-metabolites, these allowances represent generous margins of safety over minimum requirements.

THE FAT-SOLUBLE VITAMINS

Vitamin A

One of the earliest turkey studies on vitamin A was conducted by Guilbert and Hinshaw in 1934 who found that baby turkeys have poor ability to utilize beta-carotene as a dietary source of vitamin A activity. They found very little vitamin A liver storage in young poults receiving 8% alfalfa meal; but liver storage of the vitamin improved rapidly as the turkeys grew older, indicating that after a certain age, turkeys develop the enzymes needed to split beta-carotene into vitamin A, but have little of this enzyme during the critical early starting period. This poor utilization of beta-carotene by young poults was confirmed by Gurcay and associates (1948).

Early studies indicated that young poults required between 6000 and 17,000 I.U. of vitamin A/kg of diet for normal growth and freedom from deficiency signs. These very high requirement levels must have been due to poor stability of the vitamin A preparation used in the experiments, since later studies, with nutritionally complete diets all show considerably lower levels as the minimum vitamin A requirements of turkeys.

Stoewsand and Scott (1961) studied the vitamin A requirements of both breeding turkeys and their progeny. Although 2640 I.U. vitamin A/kg of breeder diet was adequate for optimum egg production, hatchability and maintenance of body weight in the hens, a level of 3520 I.U. gave better carry-over of vitamin A into the newly-hatched progeny. Poults required approximately 5200 I.U. vitamin A/kg of diet for satisfactory liver storage and minimum blood uric acid levels. These results were confirmed by Jensen (1965) and by Couch et al.(1971). Dorr and Balloun (1973) reported that better results were obtained in young poults fed

Table 4.1 Vitamin allowances

Vitamin	Starting	Growing	Finishing	Breeding
Stabilized A (added)[1,2]	10,000	4000	4000	10,000
D_3 (added)[1,2]	3600	1800	1000	3000
E acetate (added)[1,2]	25	12	5	40
K (added)[1,3]	2	2	2	2
B_1 (total)[3]	2	2	2	2
B_2 (total)[3]	7	5	4	6
Pantothenic acid (total)[3]	20	15	12	25
Niacin (added)[3]	80	65	40	40
B_6 (total)[3]	6	4.5	4	6
Biotin (total)[3]	0.3	0.25	0.15	0.25
Folic acid (total)[3]	1.2	1.0	0.9	1.25
B_{12} (added)[3]	0.015	0.01	0.007	0.015
Choline (total)[3]	2000	1750	1350	1350

[1] Addition of ethoxyquin antioxidant, 113 mg/kg diet, recommended to help prevent the loss of these vitamins.

[2] I.U./kg diet

[3] mg/kg diet

4000 I.U. vitamin A than with either 1000 or 16,000 I.U./kg of diet. The highest level of vitamin A depressed plasma inorganic phosphorus levels in all experiments. Addition of ascorbic acid to these diets did not influence either vitamin A requirements or bone mineralization.

In consideration of all of the above studies, the vitamin A allowance for breeding turkeys and for starting poults has been set at 10,000 IU/kg of diet (Table 4.1).

Vitamin D

Recent discoveries concerning vitamin D metabolism may have far-reaching beneficial effects in turkey nutrition. It is now known that vitamin D_3 *per se* is not active in the performance of any of the vitamin D functions, but must first be converted in the liver to 25-hydroxy vitamin D_3, whereupon this product is further converted, in the kidney, to 1,25-dihydroxy vitamin D_3 which is the active metabolite responsible for calcium absorption and other functions in the body (Kodicek, 1974; Norman, 1979; Schnoes and De Luca, 1980).

Robertson, Rhian and Wilhelm (1941) studied poults of turkey hens which had received graded, increasing levels of vitamin D in the breeding diet. They found that the vitamin D level in the breeding diet was all-important during the first two weeks of the starting period. After that, the vitamin D content of the poult starting diet exerted its influence on growth and calcification. Growth and calcification in poults fed a vitamin D-free diet was directly proportional, during the first four weeks, to the vitamin D level in the diet of the dams. Similar results were found in studies by Stadelman, et al.(1950) and by Stevens, et al. (1984b).

Stevens and co-workers found, using a composite mixture of poults hatched from eggs of hens that had received varying levels of vitamin D_3 (0, 300, 900, or 2700 I.U./kg of breeder diet), that no significant difference in poult weight was obtained at twelve days of age when the poults received either 900 or 2700 I.U. vitamin D_3/kg of diet. However, by the 46th day, the poults fed 2700 I.U. vitamin D_3 were more than twice as heavy as those poults receiving 900 I.U. vitamin D_3/kg of starter diet.

Moriuchi and DeLuca (1974) showed the presence of adequate levels of liver vitamin D-25-hydroxylase and kidney 25-hydroxy-vitamin D-1-hydroxylase in chicken embryos by the 18th day of incubation. Fraser and Emtage (1976) found that 90% of the D vitamin activity in the chicken egg is present as vitamin D_3 and only 5% as 25-hydroxy-vitamin D_3. It appears possible, however, that the newly hatched poult may differ from the chick and may not yet have developed the enzyme system needed for the formation of 25-hydroxy vitamin D. Therefore, the newly-hatched poult may require a greater carry-over of this vitamin D derivative from the breeding hen into the egg and the embryo, sufficient to last, not only until the poult hatches, but also well into the starting period.

Whether the form of the vitamin in the egg (and thus carried over into the newly hatched poult) is vitamin D_3 or is a hydroxylated derivative, the evidence remains that a good carry-over of vitamin D activity is important in young poults (Stevens, et al., 1984a, 1984b). It is possible, also, that under certain conditions, older turkeys may not be able to produce these vitamin D metabolites at a rate sufficient to provide the rapidly-growing turkeys with adequate bone structure, thereby producing a condition termed "vitamin D-refractory rickets". (De Luca, 1980; Hurwitz et al., 1973; Bar et al., 1987).

Symptoms of vitamin D deficiency include poor growth, awkwardness of gait, rubbery beaks, weakness of the legs (and rubbery legs in very young poults), ruffled feathers, and increased mortality. The tibia and femur show markedly reduced bone ash. Vitamin D-deficient poults with weak legs and rubbery beaks are shown in Figures 4.1 and 4.2, respectively.

Vitamin D requirements have been studied by numerous workers. Some have reported the requirement of starting poults to be approximately 800-900 I.U./kg of diet (Olsson, 1950; NRC (1984). Using several criteria of measurement (relative bone mineral mass, determined by radio-active iodine absorptiometry, bone ash determination and breaking strength of the bones), Cantor, et al. (1980) compared levels of 0, 300, 900 or 1200 I.U. vitamin D_3 per kg of diet in poult diet to 4 weeks of age. All measurements showed improved calcification of the bones with increasing levels up to 1200 I.U. vitamin D/kg of diet. Photon absorptiometry was found to be as accurate and precise as determination of bone ash for assessing bone calcification.

The studies of Stevens, et al. (1984a,b) indicate that a level of 2700 I.U. vitamin D_3/kg of diet provides an important margin of safety both in the diet of the breeding turkey hens and in the diet of the starting poults. No evidence has been obtained of any detrimental effects from this level of vitamin D_3.

Care must be taken in the selection of the vitamin D supplement to be used in diets for turkeys. Early studies by Boucher (1944) and by McGinnis and Carver (1946) showed wide variations in the activities of cod liver oil, salmon oil and irradiated animal sterols as vitamin D sources for poults. McGinnis and Carver demonstrated that the poult, like the chick, could not make use of irradiated ergosterol (vitamin D_2).

Yang, et al. (1973), in an effort to determine a possible cause of unexplained cases of rickets in turkeys, undertook a large

Figure 4.1 A vitamin D-deficient poult (left). The poults at the right received the same diet supplemented with vitamin D_3 at a level of 1000 IU/kg.

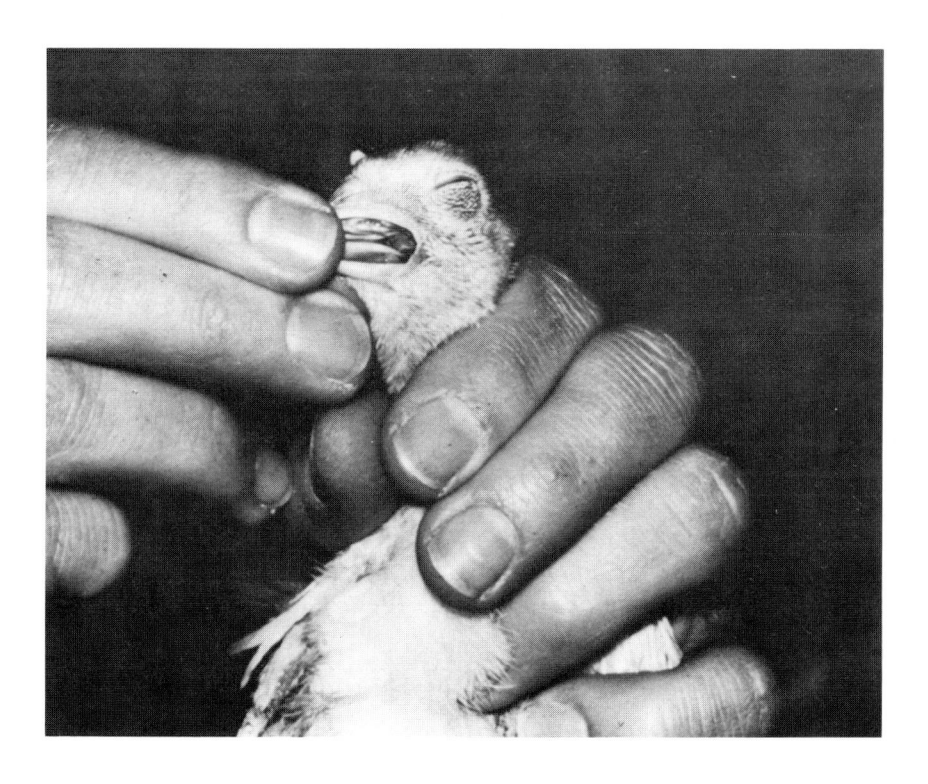

Figure 4.2 The "rubbery beak" of a vitamin D-deficient poult can be easily twisted from side to side.

evaluation of vitamin D_3 supplements used in commercial feeds for turkeys. In the first study, twenty-six supplements were assayed in young poults, using bone ash as the bioassay criterion of measurement. The samples also were assayed by means of the USP chemical assay procedure. Four samples were found to have low biopotencies. Compared to their guaranteed values, these samples had 38.9, 40.1, 41.9, and 55.8% of the stated potencies. On the other hand, the chemical assays of these samples indicated that they contained 223, 91, 85 and 114% of the guaranteed values. In a second study of 22 commercial vitamin D_3 supplements, these workers found nine samples to have much lower biopotencies than their stated values.

This demonstrates that 1) the chemical assay cannot be used to determine biologically-active vitamin D for turkeys. The bioassay should be conducted only with young poults; and 2) some commercial samples of vitamin D do not contain the guaranteed level of vitamin D-activity for young poults.

In view of all of these factors which may alter the vitamin D nutrition of turkeys, generous margins of safety have been used in setting the vitamin D_3 allowances, especially for breeders and for starting poults (Table 4.1)

Vitamin E

Although vitamin E was first discovered as a factor required for normal reproduction in both males and females, the first publication of a study of vitamin E deficiency in turkeys reported the occurence of muscular dystrophy of the gizzard in young poults fed a diet thought to be adequate in all required nutritional factors except for vitamin E (Jungherr and Pappenheimer, 1937). This disorder of young turkeys is now known to be largely due to a deficiency of selenium (Chapter 3). Vitamin E appears to act, in this case, only by sparing the selenium requirement.

Vitamin E is nature's best fat-soluble anti-oxidant. It appears to have its beneficial effects in animals and birds, such as the turkey, by helping to prevent dangerous peroxidations in the cells and organelles (mitochondria and microsomes). This helps to protect the animal from serious metabolic changes, such as damage to the brain (encephalomalacia), to the capillaries of the blood vessel system (exudative diathesis) or to the muscles of the gizzard, heart or voluntary muscle system (nutritional muscular dystrophy). Details concerning the actions of vitamin E in animals are presented in the text, "Nutrition of the Chicken", by Scott, Nesheim and Young (1982).

Following the studies of the author (1953) showing that vitamin E and niacin were helpful in preventing an "enlarged hock disorder" (see Figure 4.4) in young poults, Jensen and associates (1953, 1956) undertook experiments to determine the effects of these vitamins in breeding turkey hens. While added niacin had no effect on egg production or hatchability, vitamin E supplementation of a practical breeding diet brought about a significant improvement in hatchability. The vitamin E requirement of the breeding hens appeared to be in excess of 30 I.U./kg of diet. Vitamin E additions did not improve egg production or efficiency of feed utilization, but did improve the quality of the newly-hatched poults as evidenced by early growth and liveability.

In further studies, Jensen and McGinnis (1956) reported the vitamin E requirement of breeding turkey hens to lie between 26 and 53 I.U./kg of diet. Jensen, Carver and McGinnis (1956) reported that addition of fish liver oil to the vitamin E-low turkey breeder diet greatly accentuated the deficiency of the vitamin. Addition of either vitamin E or an antioxidant, diphenyl-para-phenylene diamine (DPPD), counteracted the deleterious effect of the fish liver oil. Also, additions of vitamin E to practical turkey breeding diets were shown by Atkinson and Couch (1954) to consistently improve hatchability in breeding turkeys.

Atkinson and associates (1955) reported that addition of 44 I.U. vitamin E/kg of diet increased hatchability of eggs of Beltsville Small White turkey hens from 51.7% on the basal diet to 88% with added vitamin E. These workers reported that vitamin E deficient turkey embryos are smaller than normal, show a cloudy lens, a cloudy, bulging cornea and appear to be blind. The peak of embryonic mortality was found to lie between the 24th and the 28th day of incubation. In 1960, Ferguson and associates reported that histologic examinations of the vitamin E-deficient embryos showed extensive liquefaction of the lens proteins and focal degeneration of the cornea, often accompanied by the formation of actual bilateral cataracts.

It is quite apparent that vitamin E is of great importance for breeding turkeys and their progeny. The recommended allowances for breeding and starting turkeys, shown in Table 4.1, provide good margins of safety over minimum requirements under normal commercial conditions.

<u>Vitamin K</u>

The "anti-hemorrhagic" vitamin K is required in higher amounts by turkeys than by chicks. Furthermore, it appears that the synthetic forms of the vitamin (menadione and its derivatives) are not as well utilized by young poults as is natural vitamin K_1 (phylloquinone). Also, though phylloquinone is stored to some extent in the egg, and thus is carried over to the newly-hatched poult, menadione does not appear to be deposited in the egg.

Much of the original research on vitamin K in turkeys was conducted in 1957. That year, Griminger presented two reports and Perdue, et al. (1957) presented a paper showing the relative biopotencies of the various commercially-available forms of vitamin K activity. They were in fairly good agreement that the vitamin K requirement of young poults, for normal blood clotting, is about 0.8 mg/kg of diet as menadione sodium bisulfite complex.

However, true vitamin K_1 was twice as potent, showing a requirement of only 0.4 mg/kg of diet.

Although vitamin K is synthesized by the intestinal microflora in humans and in many animals, Griminger (1957) could find little or no vitamin K in turkey excretions, indicating that intestinal biosynthesis of vitamin K cannot play an important role in vitamin K nutrition of turkey poults.

Vitamin K is notoriuosly unstable in premixes or in mixed feeds that have been stored for any appreciable length of time. The recommended allowance for vitamin K given in Table 4.1 represents a generous margin over minimum requirements. It is, however, recommended also that feed manufacturers take every precaution to make certain that the vitamin K preparation being used contains the stated biopotency.

In view of the much better utilization by turkeys of natural phylloquinone, it appears desirable to include a source of natural vitamin K in the diets of breeding turkey hens and young poults. Dehydrated alfalfa meal is the best feed source of this vitamin. A level of one to two percent alfalfa meal appears to contain sufficient phylloquinone for normal blood clotting in young poults; it may be desirable to use 3-5% alfalfa meal in turkey breeder diets in order to provide a good carry-over of phylloquinone into the egg.

Effects of mycotoxins on utilization of fat-soluble vitamins

Evidence is accumulating which indicates that mycotoxins in feed or litter, when consumed by turkeys cause changes that interfere with the absorption and/or utilization of the fat-soluble vitamins. When mycotoxins are unavoidably present, it may be desirable to use additional margins of safety in providing for the fat-soluble vitamin requirements of turkeys.

THE WATER-SOLUBLE VITAMINS

Of all of the nine important water-soluble vitamins, only vitamin B_{12} is stored to any appreciable extent in the livers of animals. Since these factors act as important parts of enzyme systems essential for growth and maintenance, the turkey must receive all of the required amounts of each of these vitamins on a regular basis, daily.

Although these vitamins are not stored in the liver, they are transferred from the breeding hen into the egg, approximately in proportion to the amounts of each present in the diet.

Therefore, these water-soluble vitamins are carried over into the newly-hatched poults--and this is very important for the best possible early growth of the poults.

Thiamin

Thiamin, also known as vitamin B1, is present in adequate amounts for chickens, turkeys and other animals in the normal feedstuffs that make up the bulk of the ration.

Studies by Robenalt (1960) and by Sullivan, et al. (1967) demonstrated that the thiamin requirement of turkey poults for maximum growth, freedom of signs of deficiency and maximum livability is no greater than 2.0 mg/kg of diet. In view of the fact that corn, milo, barley, wheat, brown rice, alfalfa meal, soybean meal and all other common plant feedstuffs, contain more than 3.0 mg B1/kg, it is highly unlikely that a deficiency of this vitamin will be encountered under normal commercial conditions.

However, some circumstances could lead to a deficiency. For example, meat and bone meal is almost devoid of thiamin. Coconut oil meal also is a poor source. Diets containing high levels of these ingredients, presumably might require supplementation with thiamin.

Furthermore, thiamin is readily destroyed by several different means. One of the most common causes of thiamin destruction occurs when raw fish meal is added to the diet. Raw fish contains an enzyme, termed "thiaminase" that destroys the vitamin. Thiaminase is also present in many other materials. In in many other materials. In instances in which the diet contains some unusual feedstuffs, it is possible that these feedstuffs may contain thiaminase. Other than raw fish, none of the feedstuffs usually used in variousa parts of the world contain appreciable quantities of thiaminase.

Bisulfite ions also destroy thiamin. Some instances have occured in which the sulfite content of the drinking water was high enough to bring about a thiamin deficiency in poultry. A field case in young poults, of unknown etiology, is shown in Figure 4.3.

Unless turkeys are exposed to one of the thiamin-destructive phenomena mentioned above, the recommended allowances given in Table 4.1 are adequate.

Caution must be taken in adding thiamin to poult starting and growing diets when Amprolium is used as the coccidiostat. This drug inhibits growth and development of coccidia by interfering

Figure 4.3 Commercially-reared poults showing typical "star-gazing" attribute of thiamin deficiency. This problem, of unknown etiology, was corrected by adding thiamin to the diet.

with their thiamin metabolism. If thiamin is added to such diets, this presents the coccidia with sufficient of this vitamin so that they can thrive and cause severe coccidiosis.

Riboflavin

Riboflavin, or vitamin B2, is present in large amounts in milk products; soybean meal is a fair source, as is alfalfa meal; but none of the usual gross feedstuffs are adequate to meet the requirements of starting poults or breeding turkey hens. This vitamin, therefore, must be added to all diets for turkeys.

Lepkovsky and Jukes (1936) were first to describe symptoms in poults, definitely known to be due to riboflavin deficiency, and to demonstrate that these symptoms were curable by addition to the diet of pure, crystalline riboflavin. In these early experiments, the riboflavin-deficient poults did not develop "curled toes", as occurs in riboflavin-deficient chicks, but did develop an acute dermatitis, poor growth and markedly poorer efficiency of feed utilization compared to the poults receiving the crystalline riboflavin. It appears that the diets used by Lepkovsky and Jukes were so deficient that death occurred before the "curled toe" syndrome appeared. Richardson found that a chronic riboflavin deficiency in rapidly-growing Broad Breasted Bronze poults caused severely curled toes by 35 days of age. This was prevented by giving the poults adequate riboflavin. The onset of riboflavin deficiency in poults is different from that in chicks in that a dermatitis (not seen in chicks) appears at about eight days of age. This is characterized by an inflamed and encrusted vent accompanied by excoriation in the vent area. Curled toes occur later.

Boucher, et al. (1941,1942) found that the riboflavin requirement of turkey breeding hens and starting poults is approximately 3.5 mg/kg of diet. Turkey hens receiving the basal diet containing 1.55 mg riboflavin/kg, showed no effect of the deficiency upon body weights, egg production, fertility or mortality, but the hatchability of the fertile eggs dropped to zero in a very short time of feeding the basal diet. Hatchability improved in direct proportion to the increasing levels of riboflavin up to a level of 3.0 mg riboflavin/kg of diet. Time of embryonic death advanced as the degree of deficiency became more severe. This dramatic effect of riboflavin deficiency upon hatchability was confirmed by Ferguson, et al. (1961).

Bird, et al. (1946) reported the riboflavin requirement of poults to be approximately 3.75 mg/kg of diet. They indicated that a deficiency caused perosis and that the dermatitis of riboflavin deficiency is further complicated by a biotin deficiency. McGinnis and Carver (1946) found riboflavin to be much more important than biotin in the prevention of dermatitis in young poults. McGinnis, et al. (1949) found that addition of adequate riboflavin to the poult diet helped to overcome a special type of dermatitis apparently caused by sticky droppings resulting from the use of heat-damaged soybean meal in the poult diet.

The need for adequate riboflavin supplementation of all turkey rations is now well recognized by all concerned with the feeding of turkeys. The riboflavin allowances shown in Table 4.1 represent generous margins of safety over minimum requirements.

Niacin

Niacin, also known as nicotinic acid, is of particular importance in diets of young turkeys. Special attention must be given to niacin because of two important phenomena.

1) Although almost all animals possess the ability to synthesize niacin from the amino acid, tryptophan, the turkey is a relatively poor converter of this amino acid to niacin (see the text, "Nutrition of the Chicken", pp.210-212, for details of this conversion and the reason for the relative inability of turkeys to perform the conversion).

2) Although many common feedstuffs contain quite high levels of niacin, a large part of this niacin is present in bound forms not available for digestion and absorption by turkeys.

Soon after niacin was shown to be the factor required to prevent pallagra in humans, numerous studies were conducted to determine the effects of niacin deficiency in various animals and birds.

Snell and Quarles (1941) found that the developing chick embryo contained more niacin than was present in the original egg before incubation, thereby demonstrating the net synthesis of niacin even by the embryo. This was confirmed by Schweigert et al. (1948). These studies led everyone to the conclusion that birds do not require a dietary source of niacin.

However, in 1946 Briggs showed that poults receiving highly purified diets containing all nutrients except for niacin, grew poorly and suffered inflammation of the mouth, diarrhea, poor feathering and an enlargement of the hock joint. All of these symptoms were completely prevented by supplementing the diet with 50 mg niacin/kg. Briggs indicated that higher levels of niacin may be needed for optimum growth and best efficiency of feed utilization.

Because of the high niacin content of many feedstuffs, little attention was given to a possible niacin deficiency in turkeys under practical conditions until Scott (1952,1953) found that one cause of the severe leg weaknesses being experienced by commercial turkey producers was a need to supplement practical diets with niacin. Scott found that a level of 66 mg <u>added</u> niacin per kg of diet was needed, together with added vitamin E, to completely prevent "the enlarged hock disorder" of poults receiving the basal, practical-type diet. A photograph showing the type of enlarged hocks suffered by the young poults in these studies is shown in Figure 4.4. Contrast this disorder with true perosis, which occurs in choline deficiency, shown in Figure 4.7.

As indicated previously, Jensen et al. (1953) found no effect of adding niacin to a practical turkey breeding ration. The niacin allowance recommended for breeding turkeys in Table 4.1 represents a margin of safety.

The recommended allowances for niacin given in Table 4.1 are adequate for all stages of growth, production and reproduction in turkeys. Because of the poor availability of niacin from natural feedstuffs (Kodicek, 1960; Manoukas et al., 1968), it appears desirable to add the entire requirement as supplemental niacin.

Pantothenic acid

The term "pantothenic" means "found everywhere". Thus, most feedstuffs are fairly good sources of pantothenic acid. Research indicates that only under special circumstances is it necessary to supplement chicken rations with pantothenic acid. The same was thought to be true of turkey rations.

However, in the late 1940's, Kratzer and Williams undertook studies which demonstrated that young poults require at least 10.5 mg pantothenic acid per kg of diet for normal growth, efficiency of feed utilization and prevention of symptoms characterized by severe dermatitis of the mouth and high mortality. The dermatitis of the feet, seen in pantothenic acid-deficient chicks, does not usually occur in pantothenic acid-deficient poults.

Kratzer, et al., (1955) found a relatively higher pantothenic acid requirement for normal reproduction in turkey hens. Feeding a pantothenic acid-deficient breeding diet caused hatchability of the eggs to drop to almost zero in 5 weeks. Embryos were smaller than normal and showed "wiry" down. As with chickens, borderline levels of pantothenic acid produced smaller, "mushy", baby poults and "early poult mortality" after hatching.

Approximately 16 mg pantothenic acid per kg of diet were required for optimum hatchability of high-quality poults. The levels recommended in Table 4.1 provide margins of safety for all stages of turkey production.

Figure 4.4 The "Enlarged Hock Disorder" of young poults found to be largely prevented by adequate levels of vitamin E and niacin.

Biotin

Early studies of biotin in turkey diets showed that the turkey poult has a much higher biotin requirement than the baby chick. Patrick, et al.(1942) reported that while the daily biotin requirement of chicks is only 2 micrograms, the starting poult requires two and one-half times this much, or 5 micrograms. These workers already recognized the fact that much of the biotin in some natural feedstuffs is not available to young poults and, because of the high requirement, practical rations for poults could be deficient in biotin.

Two biotin-deficient poults are shown in Figure 4.5. Symptoms include hock enlargements, dermatitis of the feet, particularly the foot pads, severe dermatitis around the eyes and mandibles and poor feathering, poor growth and death.

Waldroup and associates (1976) conducted four experiments on the possible beneficial effect of biotin upon a foot pad dermatitis of poults that has been regularly associated with a condition of the litter caused by ingredients in the diet that produce "sticky" droppings. While addition to the diet of distillers solubles (a good source of biotin) practically eliminated the foot pad dermatitis, additions of crystalline biotin did not.

Biotin has been found by many workers to be involved in a fatty liver and kidney syndrome in chicks. Thus far, no reports appear to implicate biotin in any such syndrome in turkeys.

While most studies have indicated that the biotin requirement of starting poults is no higher than 0.25 mg/kg of diet (Robblee and Clandinin, 1953, 1970; Jensen and Martinson, 1969; Waibel, et al.,1969; Dobson, 1970), Marusich, et al. (1970) reported biotin deficiency signs in poults receiving 0.25 mg biotin per kg of diet, and indicated that they believed the biotin requirement to be somewhat greater than 0.25 mg/kg diet.

As indicated in the first studies of Patrick, et al. (1942), many factors may increase the biotin requirement. Among these are the poor availablity of biotin in feedstuffs, carry-over levels of biotin from the breeding hen, effects of antibiotics and other drugs on biotin synthesis in the intestinal tract, and a destructive effect of rancidifying fats upon dietary biotin. Of these, the poor availability of biotin probably is most important. Using chick growth as the criterion, Anderson et al. (1978) reported that the biotin in wheat, barley, fish meals and meat meals is poorly available, while the biotin in corn is quite readily available.

Buenrostro and Kratzer (1984) devised an ingenious method of determining biotin requirements and availabilities of biotin in feedstuffs. They found a linear relationship between the level of

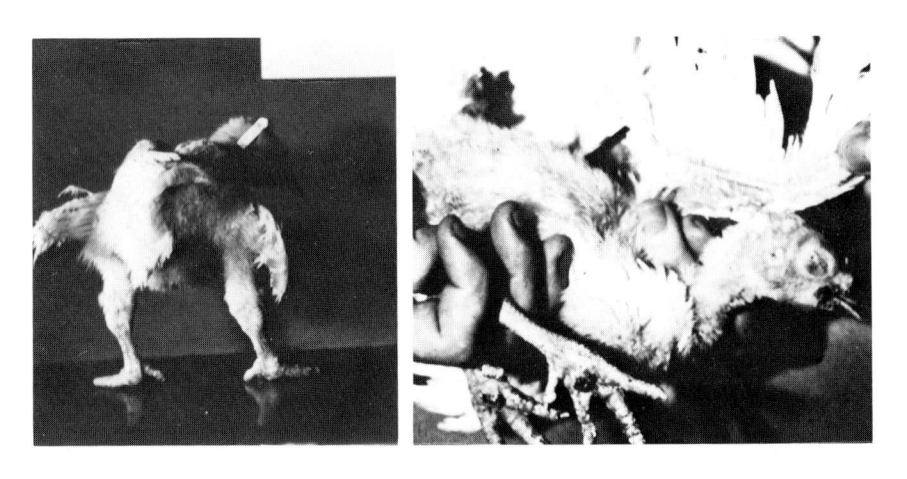

Figure 4.5 Biotin deficiency. Note severe hock enlargements (left) and dermatitis of the eyes, mandibles and feet (right).

dietary biotin and the plasma and egg yolk biotin in White Leghorn hens after feeding the diets for a period of only two weeks.

Using this method, the availability of biotin was found to be zero for wheat, 10-20% for sorghum grain (milo), 75-100% for corn, 100% for soybean meal, and 85% for meat and bone meal. Pelleting diets appeared to improve their biotin availability about 10%.

Whitehead (1984) found that the carry-over of biotin from the hen diet into the egg is directly proportional to the amount of biotin present in the diet. One reason for poor hatchability of eggs from young turkey breeders appears to be due to a relatively poor transfer of biotin to the egg at the start of egg production. This improves markedly as the hen reaches full egg production.

Holder and Sullivan (1972,1973) reported that antibiotics and sulfaquinoxaline may have important, and variable, effects upon the biotin requirement.

The discovery by Chaiet and Wolf (1964) that two strains of the mold, Streptomyces, may produce a substance termed "strepavidin" that binds biotin and renders it unavailable to animals, presents another possibly important factor that may increase the biotin requirement of turkeys. Strepavidin has been shown to be present in poultry litter.

The recommended biotin levels given in Table 4.1 are high enough to take into consideration all of the above experimental results, and to provide ample carry-over from the dam plus good margins of safety.

Pyridoxine

A deficiency of pyridoxine (vitamin B_6) in turkey poults is characterized by loss of appetite, poor growth, decreased efficiency of feed utilization, apathy, hyperexcitability when disturbed, convulsions and high mortality (Bird, et al., 1943).

The pyridoxine requirement of starting poults lies between 3.0 and 4.5 mg/kg of diet, values that are about 50% higher than the chick requirement for pyridoxine (Kratzer, et al., 1947; Armintrout et al.,1964).

In view of the high levels of pyridoxine in corn, soybean meal and other common feedstuffs, a deficiency of pyridoxine under practical conditions appears unlikely.

However, Gries and Scott (1972) showed that a border-line deficiency of pyridoxine, which is aggravated by a high protein diet, produces severe perosis in chicks. Since turkey starting diets are often exceedingly high in protein, it is desirable to make certain that the diets do indeed provide ample pyridoxine.

The levels recommended in Table 4.1 should be adequate under all types of commercial conditions.

Folic acid

In 1947, Russell, Taylor and Derby reported the folic acid requirements of young poults be approximately 2.0 mg/kg of diet.

This appears to be too high, since the studies of Scott, Heuser and Norris (1948) confirmed those of Jukes, Stokstad and Belt (1947) showing a folic acid requirement of young, starting poults of approximately 0.8 mg/kg of diet. The earlier studies may have indicated a high requirement due to very poor carry-over of folic acid in the young poults at hatching.

Lillie, Combs and Briggs (1950) found that progeny of hens fed folic acid-low practical diets showed poor growth, poor feathering, abnormal feather pigmentation and mortality regardless of the folic acid content of the chick starting diet. Saxena and associates (1954) reported that when herring meal was substituted for soybean meal as the protein supplement, poor growth, poor feathering and a high incidence of perosis occurred which was corrected by adding folic acid to the diet. It is also possible that the turkey breeding hens from which the poults were hatched were fed diets containing fish meal and little soybean and alfalfa meals, the two richest feed sources of folic acid.

Cropper and Scott (1967) demonstrated that the folic acid in soybean meal, alfalfa meal and other feedstuffs, although largely present in bound form, is fully available to turkey poults.

The folic acid requirement of breeding turkeys was found to lie between 0.7 and 1.23 mg/kg of diet (Kratzer et al., 1956; Miller and Balloun, 1967). The lower level appears to be adequate for normal hatchability, but the higher level gave best performance of the progeny. One caution arises from the finding of Lee, Belcher and Miller (1965) who reported that the folic acid content of turkey eggs showed a marked decrease when held for one week after being shipped to Iowa from the West coast.

Symptoms of folic acid deficiency in poults include poor growth, poor efficiency of feed utilization, poor feathering, depigmentation of feathering in turkeys normally having colored plumage, perosis, and severe cervical paralysis. Unlike folic acid deficient chicks, poults show very little anemia. This may be due to the fact that after deficient poults show symptoms of cervical paralysis, they die within 24 hours if not given folic acid, and thus may not live long enough to develop an anemia.

Figure 4.6 Cervical paralysis (left) in a poult receiving a folic acid-deficient diet. Note also the poor feathering. Poult at the right received the same diet supplemented with 0.8 mg folic acid/kg.

Cervical paralysis of folic acid deficiency, which appears to be unique for the turkey, is shown in Figure 4.6.

The folic acid recommendations given in Table 4.1 present a purposely high level for turkey breeders because of all of the studies indicating this to be very important. In poults hatched from turkey breeding hens receiving adequate folic acid, the allowance level indicated contains a good margin over minimum requirements.

Vitamin B_{12}

Soon after vitamin $B_{1}2$ was shown to be the "animal protein" factor, a number of studies were conducted to determine the importance of and the requirements for this vitamin in turkey nutrition.

One of the first studies (Patrick, 1951) was disappointing in that vitamin B_{12} failed to produce the same growth as was obtained from fish meal. Obviously, fish meal supplies many important nutrients (methionine and lysine, in particular) in addition to its vitamin B_{12} content.

In all efforts to determine the vitamin B_{12} requirement of starting poults, it became apparent that this vitamin is transferred from the dam to the baby poult in goodly amounts when present in high levels in the breeding diet; and that vitamin B_{12} is stored in the liver in amounts adequate to provide for the needs of the newly hatched poults for several weeks after hatching. Kratzer (1952,1953; Langer and Kratzer, 1962,1967) found that vitamin B_{12} nutrition is intimately related to the metabolism of choline, methionine and other methylated compounds in the body of turkeys, as with chicks and other animals. Vitamin B_{12} metabolism also is related to that of folic acid.

Symptoms of vitamin B_{12} deficiency, thus may be quite similar to those of a deficiency of choline, methionine or folic acid.

The vitamin B_{12} allowances given in Table 4.1 are set deliberately high because of the many important interrelationships of this vitamin in the metabolism of other factors.

Choline

From the very early work of Jukes (1942), and from many studies since then it is well established that choline is an especially important factor for turkeys. Jukes demonstrated the need for choline for the prevention of perosis in young poults. He showed that choline was the active substance in egg yolk lecithin, which had previously been shown to prevent perosis, and that methionine, inositol and creatine were completely without effect in substituting for choline.

Patrick, et al. (1943) confirmed the finding that choline is required to prevent perosis in young poults, along with biotin and some unknown factor.

Evans (1943) estimated the choline requirement of poults to lie between 0.18 and 0.25% of the diet, a level above that present in normal, practical rations. This was confirmed by Scott (1950) who found the choline requirement to depend somewhat upon the glycine content of the diet, but to be approximately 0.2% of the diet.

The perosis of choline deficiency in poults is shown in Figure 4.7.

Balloun and Miller (1964) reported the choline requirement of breeding turkeys to be no higher than 0.1% of the diet, a level well below that provided by the normal ingredients in a practical breeder ration. In view of the high amount of lecithin (and thus, of choline) in the egg, it is apparent that adult turkeys have developed the ability to synthesize choline. It is important that the breeding ration contain plenty of vitamin B_{12} because of the need for this vitamin in the synthesis of choline (Langer and Kratzer, 1964).

Friars, et al. (1964) reported that excess choline can have a depressing effect upon reproductive performance in turkey breeders.

The choline allowances presented in Table 4.1 are adjusted to meet requirements without being excessive.

SUMMARY OF THE VITAMINS IN TURKEY NUTRITION

Of the fourteen known vitamins, only thirteen are necessary in the diet of turkeys. Turkeys have a good ability to synthesize all of their needs for vitamin C (ascorbic acid).

Special attention must be given to ten of the vitamins in all turkey feed formulations. Only thiamin, pyridoxine and folic acid are usually provided in adequate amounts by the common fedstuffs used to provide for the energy, protein and amino acid requirements of turkeys.

Attenion also must be given to folic acid when diets contain little or no soybean meal are used since soybean meal is one of the best common sources of this vitamin.

The vitamin allowances presented in Table 4.1 have been shown to be adequate under a wide variety of environmental conditions.

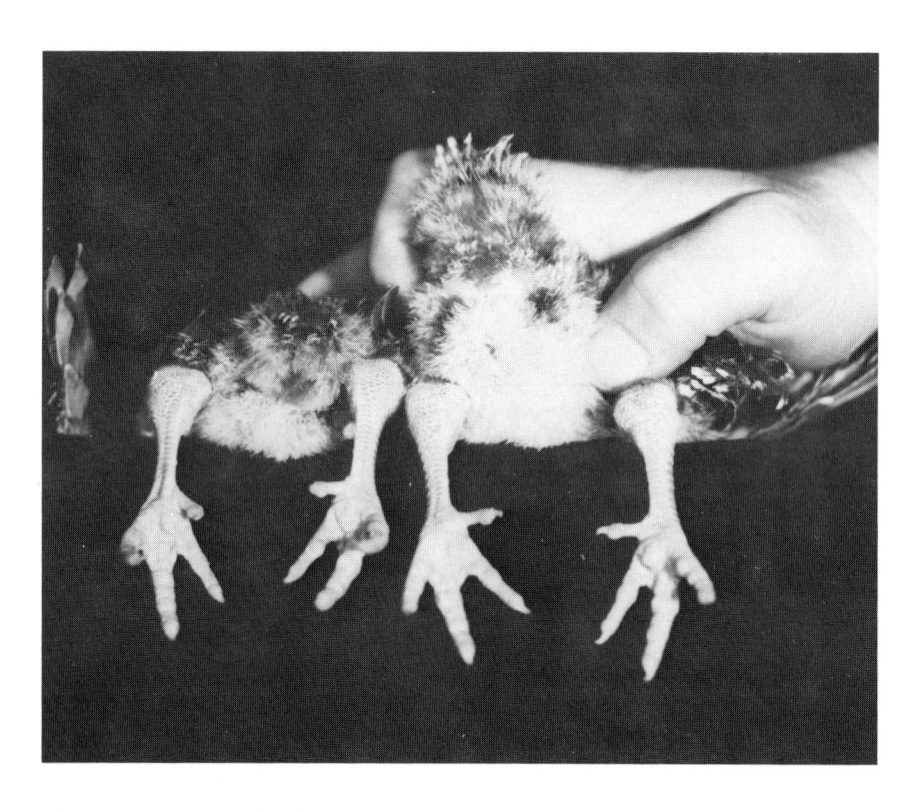

Figure 4.7   Perosis in poults suffering from choline deficiency.

REFERENCES

Anderson, J. O., and R. E. Warnick 1970. Studies of the need for supplemental biotin in chick rations. Poultry Sci. 49: 69-578.

Anderson, P. A., D. H. Baker and S. P. Mistry 1978. Bioassay determination of the biotin content of corn, sorghum and wheat. J. Animal Sci. 47: 654-659.

Arends, L. G., E. W. Kienholz, J. V. Shutze and D. D. Taylor. 1971. Effect of supplemental biotin on reproductive performance of turkey breeder hens and its effect on the subsequent progeny's performance. Poultry Sci. 50: 208-214.

Armintrout, M., H. M. Heil and T. W. Sullivan 1964. The young turkey's requirement for pyridoxine and thiamine. Poultry Sci. 43: 1301.

Atkinson, R. L., and J. R. Couch 1954. Effect of vitamin E and other supplements on hatchability of turkey eggs. Poultry Sci 33: 1039-1040.

Atkinson, R. L., T. M. Ferguson, J, Quisenberry and J. R. Couch 1955. Vitamin E and reproduction in turkeys. J. Nutrition 55: 387-397.

Balloun, S. L., and D. L. Miller 1964. Choline requirements of turkey breeder hens. Poultry Sci. 43: 64-67.

Bar, A., J. Rosenberg, R. Perlman and S. Hurwitz 1987. Field rickets in turkeys: relationship to vitamin D. Poultry Sci. 66: 68-72.

Biely, J., B. March and H. L. A. Tarr 1952. The effect of drying temperatures on the folic acid content of herring meal. Science 116: 249-250.

Bird, F. H., V. S. Asmundson, F. H. Kratzer and S. Lepkovsky 1946. The comparative requirement of chicks and poults for riboflavin. Poultry Sci. 25: 47-51.

Bird, F. H., F. H. Kratzer, V. S. Asmundson and S. Lepkovsky 1943. Pyridoxine deficiency in turkeys. Proc. Soc. Exp. Biol. & Med. 52: 44-45.

Boucher, R. V. 1944. Source of vitamin D determines amount of supplement required in turkey feed. Penn. Agr. Exp. Sta. Bul. 464 (Suppl.) 1: 2-8.

Boucher, R. V., F. W. Hill, H. Patrick and H. C. Knandel 1941. The riboflavin requirement of turkeys for hatchability. Poultry Sci. 20: 256-457.

Boucher, R. V., H. Patrick and H. C. Knandel 1942. The riboflavin requirement of turkeys for hatchability and growth. Poultry Sci. 21: 466.

Briggs, G. M., Jr. 1946. Nicotinic acid deficiency in turkey poults and the occurence of perosis. J. Nutrition 31: 79-84.

Bryant, R. L., and R. E. Moreng 1955. Improving fertility of turkey eggs. 2. Effect of adding vitamin E to the breeder diet. ND Agr. Exp. Sta. Bimonthly Bul. 18: 7-10.

Buenrostro, J. L., and F. H. Kratzer 1984. Use of plasma and egg yolk biotin of White Leghorn hens to assess biotin availability from feedstuffs. Poultry Sci. 63: 1563-1570.

Cantor, A. H., M. A. Musser, W. L. Bacon and A. B. Hellewell 1980. The use of bone mineral mass as an indicator of vitamin D status in turkeys. Poultry Sci. 59: 563-568.

Chaiet, L., and F. J. Wolf 1964. The properties of strepavidin, a biotin-bindig protein produced by streptomyces. Arch. Biochem. Biophys. 106: 1

Cropper, W. J., and M. L. Scott 1966. Nature of the blood folates in young chicks and poults fed pteroylmonoglutamic acid or pteroylheptaglutamates. Proc. Soc. Exp. Biol. & Med. 122: 817-820.

Cropper, W. J., and M. L. Scott 1967. Studies on folic acid nutrition in chicks and poults. Brit. Poultry Sci. 8: 65-73.

DeLuca, H. F. 1980. Some concepts emanating from a study of the metabolism and function of vitamin D. Nutrition Rev. 38: 169

Dobson, D. C. 1970. Biotin requirement of turkey poults. Poultry Sci. 49: 546-553.

Dorr, P. E., and S. L. Balloun 1973. Effect of dietary vitamin A, ascorbic acid and their interaction on turkey bone mineralization. Poultry Sci. 52: 2023.

Evans, R. J. 1943. The choline requirement of turkey poults. Poultry Sci. 22: 266-267.

Ferguson, T. M., C. H. Whiteside, C. R. Creger, M. L. Jones, R. L. Atkinson and J. R. Couch 1961. B-vitamin deficiency in the mature turkey hen. Poultry Sci. 40: 1151-1159.

Ferguson, T. M., A. A. Swanson, M. S. Couch, J. R. Couch, G. L. Feldman and R. H. Rigdon 1960. Experimental studies on cataract formation. Amer. J. Opthal. 49: 1165-1167.

Fraser, D. R., and J. S. Emtage 1976. Vitamin D in the avian egg. Its molecular identity and mechanism of incorporation into yolk. Biochem. J. 160: 671-682.

Friars, G. W., S. J. Slinger and W. F. Pepper 1964. Effect of continuous and intermittent reserpine and different choline treatments on the growth and reproductive performance of turkeys. Poultry Sci. 43: 941-946.

Gries, C. L., and M. L. Scott 1972. The pathology of pyridoxine deficiency in chicks. J. Nutrition 102: 1259

Griminger, P. 1957a. On the vitamin requirements of poults. 1. Vitamin K. Poultry Sci. 36: 1123.

Griminger, P. 1957b. On the vitamin K requirement of turkey poults. Poultry Sci. 36: 1227-1235.

Guilbert, H. R., and W. R. Hinshaw 1934. Vitamin A storage in the livers of turkeys and chickens. J. Nutrition 8: 45-56.

Gurcay, R., R. V. Boucher and E. W. Callenbach 1948. Utilization of vitamin A and beta-carotene by turkey poults. Poultry Sci. 27: 665-666.

Holder, D. P., and T. W. Sullivan 1972. The effect of terramycin, penicillin, bacitracin and sulfaquinoxaline on the biotin requirement of starting turkeys. Poultry Sci. 51: 1820.

Holder, D. P., and T. W. Sullivan 1973. Influence of folic acid, vitamin B-12 and pantothenic acid on the biotin requirement of starting turkeys. Poultry Sci. 52: 2041.

Hurwitz, S., A. Bar and A. Meshorer 1973. Field rickets in turkey poults: plasma and bone chemistry, bone histology, intestinal calcium-binding protein. Poultry Sci. 52: 1370-1374.
Jensen, L. S. 1965. Vitamin A requirement of breeding turkeys. Poultry Sci. 44: 1609-1610.
Jensen, L. S., J. S. Carver and J. McGinnis 1955. Vitamin E, diphenyl-para-phenylene-diamine and fish liver oil in turkey reproduction. Poultry Sci. 34: 1203.
Jensen, L. S., G. F. Heuser, M. L. Scott and L. C. Norris 1953. The effect of vitamin E and niacin in the nutrition of turkey breeder hens. Poultry Sci. 32: 907
Jensen, L. S., and R. Martinson 1969. Requirement of turkey poults for biotin and effect of deficiency on incidence of leg weakness in developing turkeys. Poultry Sci. 48: 222
Jensen, L. S., and J. McGinnis 1956. Quantitative requirement of turkey breeder hens for vitamin E. Poultry Sci. 36:1149
Jensen, L. S., and J. McGinnis 1957. Studies on the vitamin E requirement of turkeys for reproduction. Poultry Sci. 36: 1344-1350.
Jukes, T. H. 1942. Experiments on the storage of vitamin A by growing turkeys. Poultry Sci. 21: 357-360.
Jukes, T. H., E. L. R. Stokstad and M. Belt 1947. Deficiencies of certain vitamins as studied with turkey poults on a purified diet. J. Nutrition 33: 1-12.
Jungherr, E., and A. M. Pappenheimer 1937. Nutritional myopathy of the gizzard in turkeys. Proc. Soc. Biol. & Med. 37: 520
Kodicek, E. 1960. The availability of bound nicotinic acid to the rat. Brit. J. Nutrition 14: 13; 14: 25; 14: 35.
Kratzer, F. H. 1952. The effect of vitamin B-12 upon the utilization of choline and betaine by the young poult. J. Nutrition 48:201-207.
Kratzer, F. H., F. H. Bird, V. S. Asmundson and S. Lepkovsky 1947. The comparative pyridoxine requirement of chicks and turkey poults. Poultry Sci. 26:453-456.
Kratzer, F. H., P. N. Davis and U. K. Abbott 1956. The folic acid requirements of turkey breeder hens. Poultry Sci. 35: 711-716.
Kratzer, F. H., P. N. Davis, B. J. Marshall and D. E. Williams 1955. The pantothenic acid requirement of turkey hens. Poultry Sci. 34: 68-72.
Kratzer, F. H., and D. E. Williams 1948. The pantothenic acid requirement of poults for early growth. Poultry Sci. 27: 518-523.
Langer, B. W., Jr., and F. H. Kratzer 1962. The relationship of vitamin B-12 content to methionine biosynthesis in turkey poult liver homogenates. Poultry Sci. 41: 1989-1999.
Langer, B. W., Jr., and F. H. Kratzer 1967. The vitamin B-12 formaldehyde complex as a one-carbon unit precursor in the biosynthesis of methionine in turkey poult liver homogenates. Poultry Sci. 46: 749-754.
Lee, C. D., L. V. Belcher and D. L. Miller 1965. Field

observation of folacin deficiency in poults. Avian Dis. 9: 508-512.
Lepkovsky, S., and T. H. Jukes 1936. The response of rats, chicks and turkey poults to crystalline vitamin G (flavin). J. Nutrition 12: 515-526.
Lillie, R. J., G. F. Combs and G. M. Briggs, Jr. 1950. Folic acid in poultry nutrition. II. Effect of maternal diet and chick diet upon mortality, growth and feathering of progeny. Poultry Sci. 29: 115
Manoukas, A. G., R. C. Ringrose and A. E. Terri 1968. The availability of niacin in corn, soybean meal and wheat middlings for the hen. Poultry Sci. 47: 1836
Marusich, W. L., E. F. Ogrinz, M. Brand and M. Mitrovic 1970. Induction, prevention and therapy of biotin deficiency in turkey poults on semi-purified and commercial-type rations. Poultry Sci. 49: 412-421.
McGinnis, J., and J. S. Carver 1946. The effect of riboflavin and biotin on dermatitis and perosis in turkey poults. Poultry Sci. 25: 407-408.
McGinnis, J., W. D. Graham and J. S. Carver 1949. The relation of heat-damaged soybean protein and riboflavin deficiency to dermatitis in turkey poults. Poultry Sci. 28: 774.
Miller, D. L., and S. L. Balloun 1967. Folacin requirements of turkey breeder hens. Poultry Sci. 46: 1502-1508.
Moriuchi, S. and H. F. DeLuca 1974. Metabolism of vitamin D-3 in the chick embryo. Arch. Biochem. Biophys. 164: 165-171.
NRC 1984. Nutrient requirements of poultry, 8th Ed. Revised. National Acad. Press, Washington, D. C.
Norman, A. W. 1979. <u>Vitamin D: the calcium homeostatic steroid hormone</u>. Academic Press, New York.
Olsson, N. 1950. Investigations on the vitamin D requirements of chicks, poults, ducklings and goslings. World's Poultry Sci. J. 6: 230.
Patrick, H. 1951. Vitamin B-12 and antibiotics in turkey poult nutrition. Poultry Sci. 30: 549-551.
Patrick, H., R. V. Boucher, R. A. Dutcher and H. C. Knandel 1943. Prevention of perosis and dermatitis in turkey poults. J. Nutrition 26: 197-204.
Patrick, H., R. V. Boucher, R. A. Dutcher and H. c. Knandel 1942. The nutritional significance of biotin in chick and poult nutrition. Poultry Sci. 21: 476
Perdue, H. S., H. C. Spruth and D. V. Frost 1957. The vitamin K requirements of turkey poults. Poultry Sci. 36: 1148
Robblee, A. R., and D. R. Clandinin 1953. The use of calcium pantothenate and biotin in practical poult starters. Poultry Sci 32: 579-582.
Robblee, A. R., and D. R. Clandinin 1970. The role of biotin in the nutrition of turkey poults. Poultry Sci. 49: 976-981.
Robenalt, R. C. 1960. The thiamine requirement of young turkey poults. Poultry Sci. 39: 354-360.
Robertson, E. I., M. Rhian and L. A. Wilhelm 1941. The response of poults from turkey hens fed different levels of vitamin D.

Poultry Sci. 20: 471

Russell, W. C., M. W. Taylor and J. V. Derby, Jr. 1947. The folic acid requirement of turkey poults on a purified diet. J. Nutrition 34: 621-632.

Saxena, H. C., G. E. Bearse, C. F. McClary, L. G. Blaylock and L. R. Berg 1954. Deficiency of folic acid in rations containing natural feedstuffs. Poultry Sci. 33: 815-820.

Schnoes, H. K., and H. F. DeLuca 1980. Recent progress in vitamin D metabolism and the chemistry of vitamin D metabolites. Fed. Proc. 39: 2723

Schweigert, B. S., H. L. German, P. B. Pearson and R. M. Sherwood 1948. Effect of the pteroylgutamic acid intake on the performance of turkeys and chickens. J. Nutrition 35: 89-102.

Scott, M. L. 1950. Studies on the enlarged hock disorder (perosis) in turkeys. J. Nutrition 40: 611-624.

Scott, M. L. 1952. The effect of niacin upon the enlarged hock disorder of turkeys. Poultry Sci. 31: 934

Scott, M. L. 1953. Prevention of the enlarged hock disorder of turkeys with niacin and vitamin E. Poultry Sci. 32: 670-677.

Scott, M. L., G. F. Heuser and L. C. Norris 1948. Studies in turkey nutrition using a pruified diet. Poultry Sci. 27: 770-772.

Scott, M. L., M. C. Nesheim and R. J. Young 1982. **NUTRITION OF THE CHICKEN**, M. L. Scott & Associates, P. O. Box 816, Ithaca, N. Y. 14851.

Snell, E. E., and E. Quarles 1941. The effect of incubation on the vitamin content of eggs. J. Nutrition 22:483

Stadelman, W. J., R. V. Boucher and E. W. Callenbach 1950. The effect od vitamin D in the turkey breeder ration on egg production and hatchability and on growth and calcification in the poults. Poultry Sci. 29: 146-152.

Stevens, . I., R. Blair, R. E. Salmon and J. P. Stevens 1984. Effect of varying levels of dietary vitamin D on turkey hen egg production, fertility and hatchability, embryo mortality and incidence of embryo beak malformations. Poultry Sci. 63: 760-764.

Stevens, V. I., R. Blair and R. E. Salmon 1984. Influence of maternal vitamin D-3 carry-over on kidney 25-hydroxyvitamin D-3-1-hydroxylase activity of poults. Poultry Sci. 63: 765-774.

Stoewsand, G. S., and M. L. Scott 1961. The vitamin A requirements of breeding turkeys and their progeny. Poultry Sci. 40: 1255-1262.

Sullivan, T. W., H. M. Heil and M. E. Amintrout 1967. Dietary thiamine and pyridoxine requirements of young turkeys. Poultry Sci. 46: 1560-1564.

Waibel, P. E., L. M. Krista, R. L. Arnold, L. G. Blaylock and L. H. Neagle 1969. Effect of supplementary biotin on performance of turkeys fed corn-soybean meal type diets. Poultry Sci. 48: 1979-1985.

Waldroup, P. W., J. F. Maxey, L. W. Luther, B. D. Jones and M. L. Meshew 1976. Factors affecting the response of turkeys to biotin and pyridoxine supplementation. Ark. Agr. Exp. Sta. Bul. 805.

Whitehead, C. C. 1984. Biotin intake and transfer to the egg and chick in broiler breeder hens housed on litter or in cages. Brit. Poultry Sci. 25: 287-292.

Yang, H. S., P.E. Waibel and J Brenes 1973. Evaluation of vitamin D-3 supplements by biological assay using the turkey. J. Nutrition 103: 1187-1194.

CHAPTER 5

ESSENTIAL FATTY ACIDS UNIDENTIFIED FACTORS AND ANTIBIOTICS

Linoleic and arachidonic acids are essential in turkey nutrition. The linoleic acid requirement of starting poults is approximately 1.0% of the diet for maximum growth and optimum efficiency of feed utilization (Ketola, Young and Nesheim, 1973). Linoleic acid is needed in turkey breeder diets for production of normal-sized eggs and for normal hatchability. This requirement also is no greater than 1.0% of the diet.

The requirement is given in terms of linoleic acid because this fatty acid can serve as the source of both linoleic and arachidonic acids. The body has the ability to synthesize arachidonic from linoleic acid.

Linoleic acid is synthesized by plants, but not by animals. Best sources of linoleic acid are the vegetable oils, which range in linoleic acid content from as much as 73% in safflower oil to as little as 7% in olive oil. Most vegetable oils (corn, soybean, cottonseed, sunflower oils) contain about 50% linoleic acid. Acidulated soapstock also is a good source, containing about 45% linoleic acid. Lecithin usually contains linoleic acid in the number 2 position of the molecule, thus representing about 30% of this phospholipid, while the linoleic acid content of lard is only 10%. The commercial product known as soya lecithin was shown by Bonomi and Bianchi (1972) to produce better poult growth and efficiencies of feed utilization than lard when both were fed at 0.5 and 1.0% of the diet.

Although not synthesized by animals, linoleic acid is stored in the fats and phospholipids of all animals, where it may be found in quite high amounts, depending upon the diet fed to the animal.

Several investigations have been conducted to determine the essential fatty acid composition of the egg, the embryo and the tissues of turkeys of different ages and of the effects of different diets upon the amounts and proportions of the various fatty acids in turkeys and turkey eggs.

Christie and Moore (1972) found the lipids in eggs of 23 avian species to be remarkably similar; triglycerides ranged from 61 to 72%, while phosphatidylcholine (lecithin) represented about 24% and phosphatidylethanolamine was about 4.5% of the total lipid. Couch and Saloma (1973) reported on the fatty acid positional distribution in the lipids of egg yolks of turkeys and other species of domestic and game birds. They found the linoleic acid predominantly linked in the 2-position of both the triglycerides and the phosphatides.

Cornett (1972), in studies of the fatty acid composition of turkey embryos, found that during the first ten days of incubation, these embryos used more linoleic and other polyunsaturated fatty acids than saturated or monounsaturated fatty acids, thus providing a possible reason for the importance of adequate linoleic acid for normal hatchability of turkey eggs.

Neudoerffer and Lea (1966, 1967, 1968) studied the effects of dietary polyunsaturated fatty acids, particularly fish oils, on the individual lipid composition of turkey breast and leg muscle.

FATTY ACIDS IN TISSUES

The turkeys given fish oil contained seven major and two minor fatty acids derived from the fish oil, not present in the lipids of the control group. Most of these fatty acid were present in the skin fats at about 1/2 to 2/3 of their concentrations in the dietary lipid. While the turkeys deposited most of the fatty acid unchanged, they also appeared to concentrate certain fatty acid from the fish oil. Docosahexanoic acid (22:6) reached a concentration nearly five times as great as its concentration in the dietary lipids. Hydrolysis with phospholipase A showed that most of these polyunsaturated fatty acids were present in the number 2 position of the phospholipids.

Carlson and associates (1969) found that turkeys receiving corn oil had a 25% relative increase in the linoleic acid content of the carcass fatty acids with concomitant decreases in oleic and palmitoleic acids. Salmon and O'Neil (1973) found that the composition of the depot fat of turkeys resembled the dietary fat during the rapid growth phase, but toward the end of the finishing period this fat showed increases in stearic, oleic and palmitoleic acids, indicating an increase in biosynthesis of body fats from carbohydrates.

These findings help to explain the marked improvement in efficiency of feed utilization that accrues from the use of high dietary fat levels in growing and finishing diets for turkeys. This a direct function of dietary fat, over and above its need as a source of essential fatty acids.

While the essential fatty acid requirements of both poults and breeding turkeys can be met by a level of approximately 1.0% linoleic acid, the level of fat that promotes best efficiency of feed utilization is much greater--in the neighborhood of 5-10% dietary fat.

UNIDENTIFIED FACTORS IN TURKEY NUTRITION

Possible need for linolenic acid (omega-3 fatty acids)

Fish and other aquatic species are known to require a fatty acid of the omega-3 series, such as linolenic or one of the fish oil fatty acids. The finding of Neudoerffer and Lea (1968) that turkeys concentrate docosahexanoic acid in their tissues may indicate a special need for this series of fatty acids.

Lands (1982) has reported observations on the effect of fish oil fatty acids upon prostaglandin synthesis in animals. Goodnight (1981), Brox, et al. (1981) and Ahmed et al. (1984) reported effects of omega-3 fatty acids upon platelet formation.

No evidence has been reported thus far indicating that these fatty acids have been studied in turkeys. Reports persist, however, on the possible existence of unidentified growth and hatchability factors in fish meals and fish solubles for turkeys.

Possible unidentified factor/factors in fish solubles

Over the thirty years since the discovery of selenium as a nutrient, and with the full knowledge of the importance of vitamin B_{12}, numerous reports have appeared in the literature indicating a need for an as yet unidentified factor or factors in fish meal and fish solubles for both growth and normal reproduction in turkeys.

Using basal, practical diets composed largely of corn and soybean meal, or sorghum grain and soybean meal, various workers have consistently found small, but important increases in growth, improved hatchability of fertile eggs and efficiency of feed utilization upon addition of fish meal or fish solubles to the diet (Chu, 1968; Anderson and Warnick, 1970; Atkinson, et al., 1970; Chang and Waibel, 1970; Touchburn et al., 1974).

No explanations were put forth by these workers as to the possible causes of these improvements. In one study, however, Harms (1973) reported that addition of inorganic sulfate to the poult diet promoted a response equivalent to that obtained with fish solubles. Harms suggested that the unidentified growth response to fish solubles may be due to its sulfate content. But in another experiment by Sloan and Harms (1972) and in studies by Potter, et al. (1983) and Blair, et al., (1986), no responses were obtained from adding sulfate to turkey diets that were adequate in methionine.

Since, in most of the studies on unidentified factors required by turkeys, special efforts were made to assure adequacy of all known nutrients, it still appears that fish solubles contain some unknown growth-promoting activity.

One of the difficulties encountered in the studies of unidentified factors having only small effects, is the possibility that the source of the unknown activity is simply having a beneficial effect upon the palatability of the diet. This effect must be ruled out before one can be certain of the existence in fish meals and fish solubles of a "vitamin" or other such factor that can be isolated, identified and added to the list of required nutrients.

Even if the unidentified activity in fish meal and fish solubles is found to be an effect upon palatability, this would make it none the less important in terms of the economic improvements in results obtained through the use of these products in practical rations for turkeys.

Studies have indicated the existence of "unidentified factor" activity also in plant materials. Several investigations have indicated the possible existence of unknown required factors in soybean meal, in alfalfa meal, in dried fermentation solubles and, particularly, in dried brewer's yeast (Sweet, 1956; Whiteside, et al., 1960; Jensen and McGinnis, 1961; Bonsembiante and Parigi, 1973).

Several studies in the author's laboratory and elsewhere showed that relatively poor growth of young poults occured on purified diets in which synthetic amino acids were used at supposedly adequate levels together with adequate levels of all other required nutrients. Growth was markedly improved by substitution of soybean meal, keeping the levels of all essential amino acids constant.

Kratzer, et al. (1959) attempted to isolate the growth and antiperotic factors from soybean meal. The factors could be extracted by methanol, but were shown not to be similar to lecithin or other phospholipid. The factors also were shown to be present in egg yolk.

Wilcox (1960) found a large difference in growth of poults receiving protein from soybean meal, compared to that of those receiving the same diet in which the soybean meal was replaced by isolated, purified soybean protein. Griffith and Young (1966) also reported a similar growth response when soybean meal replaced isolated soy protein in the diet of poults. Blair, et al. (1972) demonstrated the existence in soybeans of an unknown factor that improved the growth of baby quail by 50% over that obtained with a purified diet formulated to be complete in all known nutrients. Fortunately, almost all present-day turkey rations contain much more soybean meal than that found by Blair et al. to be required for maximum growth responses.

The factor in dried brewer's yeast will be discussed in greater detail in the following chapter dealing with leg weaknesses and other nutritional anomalies of turkeys.

The grass juice factor

In studies of the "alfalfa" factor, it was found (Scott, 1951) that the juices prepared commercially from alfalfa or cereal grasses possessed marked growth-stimulating activities for young poults. The probable explanation of this response will be discussed below under the subject of antibiotics and chemotherapeautic agents.

ANTIBIOTICS AND CHEMOTHERAPEAUTIC AGENTS AS GROWTH FACTORS

Following the report of Stokstad and Jukes (1950) showing that crystalline aureomycin, at a very low level in the diet, produced a marked growth response, countless studies in numerous laboratories demonstrated that this effect occured consistently on all types of diets.

Several workers also found that antibiotic supplementation of turkey breeder rations produced some improvements in egg production, broodiness, and efficiency of feed utilization, especially during periods of heat stress (Muller et al., 1961; Deacon and Patterson, 1966).

The diets used in the early 1950's were not as nutriionally complete, and apparently the environmental "disease level" was rather high at that time, such that the feeding of an antibiotic often produced a growth response of as much as 50% increase over the growth of the poults receiving the basal diet.

All of the known antibiotics appeared to have approximately equal activity (Branion and Hill, 1951). Furthermore, it was found that the organic arsenic compounds, arsanilic acid and 3-nitro,4-hydroxyphenyl arsonic acid, and copper sulfate, produced growth responses that were similar to the responses to antibiotics.

Because the unabsorbable antibiotics, such as bacitracin, were as effective as the absorbable ones, such as penicillin and the tetracyclines, it was early apparent that the growth-promoting activities of these substances were acting in the intestinal tracts of the turkeys. As management conditions improved, and the environment became "cleaner", growth on the basal diets improved remarkably and the growth response, though still evident in most instances, was more in the order of 10% rather than the large responses indicated with the early use of antibiotics.

Forbes, Supplee and Combs (1958) demonstrated that germ-free poults fed purified diets without antibiotic supplementation grew as well as those fed a conventional diet with antibiotics. Addition of either penicillin or oleandamycin to the germ-free diet did not improve growth above that obtained without the antibiotic.

Copper sulfate and the grass juice factor

Some time after Barber et al. (1955) reported that a high dietary level of copper sulfate had a marked growth-promoting effect in pigs, Scott and Peter (1965) conducted an intensive study with turkey poults, comparing the growth-promoting effect of copper sulfate with that of several different antibiotics. It was found that a level of 50 mg copper as copper sulfate per kg of diet promoted the same growth response in the poults as was obtained with the various antibiotics, and that the addition of the antibiotics to the copper treatment produced no better growth response than that obtained with either alone.

This finding provided an explanation for the growth-promoting effect of the commercial grass and alfalfa juices referred to above. It was known that these juices had been preserved by addition of 5% copper sulfate which was sufficient to provide 50 ppm copper when the grass juices were used at the level of 5% in the diet.

SUMMARY REGARDING ESSENTIAL FATTY ACIDS, UNIDENTIFIED FACTORS AND ANTIBIOTICS FOR TURKEYS

Starting poults and turkey breeding hens require approximately 1% linoleic acid for optimum growth, efficiency of feed utilization, optimum egg production and maximum egg size. Arachidonic acid can substitute for part of this requirement. It is possible, though not proven, that turkeys may also require a small amount of linolenic acid or another of the omega-3 fatty acids as found in fish oils.

Soybean meal, fish solubles and fermentation solubles may contain unidentified nutritional factors required for maximum growth in turkeys. However, the possiblity exists that the growth responses observed when these materials are added to complete diets are due to positive effects upon palatability of the diets.

Addition of a wide variety of antibiotics or copper sulfate to diets of young poults at a level of 50 ppm usually produces a growth increase compared with the growth obtained in the absence of the anti-microbial substance. This response is usually in the order of 10% over the control diet.

REFERENCES

Ahmed, A. A., and B. J. Holub 1984. Alteration and recovery of bleeding times, platelet aggregation and fatty acid composition of individual phospholipids in platelets of human subjects receiving a supplement of cod liver oil. Lipids 19: 617

Anderson. J. O., and R. E. Warnick 1970. Effect of replacing part of the soybean meal in turkey poult rations with amino acid and carbohydrate mixtures. Poultry Sci. 49: 459-467.

Atkinson, R. L., J. W. Bradley, J. R. Couch and J. H. Quisenberry 1970. Condensed fish solubles in turkey nutrition. Nutrition Rpts. Intern. 2: 231-241.

Barber, R. J., R. Braude and K. C. Mitchell 1955. Antibiotics and copper supplements for fattening pigs. Brit. J. Nutrition 9: 378-381.

Blair, M. E., L. M. Potter, B. A Bliss and J. R. Shelton 1986. Methionine, choline and sulfate supplementation of practical-type diets for young turkeys. Poultry Sci. 65: 130-137.

Blair, R., M. L. Scott and R. J. Young 1972. Unidentified factor activities in whole soybeans required for optimium growth in Coturnix quail. J. Nutrition 102: 1529-1542.

Bonomi, A., and M. Bianchi 1972. Soya lecithin in feeds for turkeys. Avicultura 41: 89-95.

Bonsembiante, M. and B. R. Parigi 1973. Nutritive requirements and alimentary planes in turkey production. Rivista di aviculura 42: 41-50.

Branion, H. D., and D. C. Hill 1951. The comparative effect of antibiotics on the growth of poults. Poultry Sci. 30: 793-798.

Brox, J. H., J. E. Killie, S. Gunnes and A. Nordoy 1981. The effect of cod liver oil and corn oil on platelets and vessel wall in man. Thrombosis and Haemeostasis 46: 604

Carlson, C. W., E. Guenther, K. C. Schneider, L. P. Guild, D. Deethardt and Y. A. Greichus 1969. Effects of corn oil and lysine on growth, fatty acid composition and palatability of large Broad White turkeys. Poultry Sci. 48: 1027

Chang, S. H., and P. E. Waibel 1970. Efficacy of zinc bacitracin and sources of unidentified growth factors with corn-soybean meal type diet for turkey poults. Poultry Sci. 49: 733-743.

Christie, W. W., and J. H. Moore 1972. The lipid composition and triglyceride structure of eggs from several avian species. Comp. Biochem. & Physiol. 41: 297-305.

Chu, A. B. 1968. Unknown growth factor(s), protein and fat digestibility, and metabolizable energy evaluations of fish solubles in diets of young turkeys. Diss. Abstr. B29: 868.

Cornett, B. M. 1972. Effects of dietary fat on the fatty acid composition of turkey embryos. Diss. Abstr. B32: 5604.

Couch, J. R., and A. E. Saloma 1973. Fatty acid positional distribution in egg yolk triglycerides from various avian species. Lipids 8: 675-681.

Deacon, L. E., and E. B. Patterson 1966. The effect of

oxytetracycline on the performance of turkey breeder hens. Poultry Sci. 45: 1053-1058.

Forbes, M., W. C. Supplee and G. F. Combs 1958. Response of germ-free and conventionally reared turkey poults to dietary supplementation with penicillin and oleandomycin. Proc. Soc. Exp. Biol. & Med. 99: 110-113.

Goodnight, S. H., W. S. Harris and W. E. Connor 1981. The effects of dietary omega-3 fatty acids on platelet composition and function in man: a protective, controlled study. Blood 58: 880

Griffith, M., and R, J, Young 1966. Growth response of turkey poults to fractions of soybean meal. J. Nutrition 89: 293

Harms, R. H. 1973. Formulation of feed with new and unusual products for the international market. World Poultry Sci. J. 29: 9-17.

Jensen, L. S., and J. McGinnis 1961. Nutritional investigations with turkey hens. 2. Requirement for unidentified factors. Poultry Sci. 40: 731-734.

Ketola, H. G., R. J. Young and M. C. Nesheim 1973. Linoleic acid requirements of turkey poults. Poultry Sci. 52: 597-603.

Kramke, E. H., and J. C. Fritz 1951. The response of chicks and poults to low levels of antibiotics. Poultry Sci. 30: 921.

Kratzer, F. H., P. Vohra, R. L. Atkinson, P. N. Davis, B J. Marshall and J. B. Allred 1959. Fractionation of soybean oil meal for growth and anti-perotic factors. 1. Non-phospholipid nature of the factors. Poultry Sci. 38: 1049-1055.

Lands, W. E. M. 1982. Biochemical observations on dietary long chain fatty acids from fish oil and their effect on prostaglandin synthesis in animals and human. In *Nutritional evaluation of long chain fatty acids in fish oil.* S. M. Barlow and M. E. Stansby, Eds., Academic Press, New York.

Muller, Z., J. Roedl, Z Zensek and V. Lautner 1961. Effect of penicillin on egg yield of turkey hens with reference to amounts of the most important amino acids and vitamins in the eggs for setting. World's Poultry Sci. J. 17: 371-372.

Neudoerffer, T. S., and C. H. Lea 1966. Effects of dietary fish oil on the composition and stability of turkey depot fat. Brit. J. Nutrition 20: 581-594.

Neudoerffer, T. S., and C. H. Lea 1967. Effects of dietary polyunsaturated fatty acids on the composition of the individual lipids of turkey breast and leg muscle. Brit. J. Nutrition 21: 691-714.

Neudoerffer T. S., and C. H. Lea 1968. Effects of dietary fat on the amounts and proportions of the individual lipids in turkey muscle. Brit. J. Nutrition 22: 115-128.

Pepper, W. F., and S. J. Slinger 1955. Effect of arsonic acid derivatives and a high level of aureomycin on the performance of turkeys to 24 weeks of age. Poultry Sci. 34: 928-934.

Potter, L. M., J. R. Shelton and D. J. Castaldo 1983. Supplementary inorganic sulfate and methionine for young turkeys. Poultry Sci. 62: 2398-2402.

Salmon, R. E., and J. B. O'Neil 1973. The effect of the level and source and of a change of source of dietary fat on the fatty acid composition of the depot fat and the thigh and breast meat of turkeys as related to age. Poultry Sci. 52: 302-304.

Scott, M. L. 1951. The grass juice factor in turkey nutrition. Poultry Sci. 30: 293-297.

Scott, M. L., and V. Peter 1965. Recent turkey studies with antibiotics and other anti-microbial agents. Poultry Sci. 44: 1414.

Sloan, D. R., and R. H. Harms 1972. Utilization of inorganic sulfate by turkey poults. Poultry Sci. 51: 1673-1675.

Stokstad, E. L. R., and T. H. Jukes 1950. Growth-promoting effect of aureomycin on turkey poults. Poultry Sci. 29: 611-612.

Sweet, G. B. 1956. Unidentified factors in chick, poult and hen nutrition Diss. Abstr. 16 200-201.

Touchburn, S. P., R. D. M. Silva and E. C. Naber 1974. Further evidence for an unidentified nutrient in fish solubles which improves hatchability and progeny growth of turkeys and Japanese quail. Poultey Sci. 53: 1745-1758.

Whiteside, C. H., T. M. Ferguson, B. L. Reid and J. R. Couch 1960. The effect of dehydrated alfalfa meal, condensed fish solubles and fermentation residue on the reproductive performance of turkeys. Poultry Sci. 39: 77-81.

CHAPTER 6

LEG WEAKNESSES, ASCITES, PENDULOUS CROPS, AORTIC RUPTURE AND OTHER ANOMALIES OF TURKEYS

Leg weaknesses

Many factors are known to be involved in the maintenance of normal bone structure and freedom from leg weaknesses in turkeys. Some are genetic; certains strains of turkeys have been found to be more susceptible to leg weaknesses than others. Some are due to diseases, such as the synovitis of infection with Micoplasma synoviae or Micoplasma gallicepticum, which also produce air sac disease. Only occasionally has Staphylococcic arthritis occurred in any appreciable incidence within a turkey flock. This disease is more apt to occur in an occasional turkey that has suffered an injury to the foot or hock joint, thus allowing the invasion of the Staphylococcus organisms. Outbreaks of this disease in young poults have been described by Jungherr (1933) and by Bowness and Fahey (1954). A leg deformity associated with a Salmonella enteritidis infection also has been reported (Higgins, et al., 1944).

Many times, the cause of leg weakness may be nutritional. Of the nutritional factors, some are still unidentified but many of the well established nutrients are known to be required for the prevention of leg weaknesses.

Among these are the factors necessary for bone calcification--calcium, phosphorus and vitamin D_3, and the need to convert dietary vitamin D_3 to the hormone form of the vitamin, 1,25-dihydroxy vitamin D_3. A deficiency of any of these factors, or an insufficiency in conversion of vitamin D_3, will lead to rickets. A rachitic poult was shown in Figure 3.1.

Factors known to be required for prevention of perosis are choline, biotin, folic acid, manganese and zinc. Although pyridoxine deficiency has not been shown to produce perosis in turkeys, a severe perosis has been demonstrated in broiler chicks fed diets that were only slightly deficient in pyridoxine (Gries and Scott, 1972). Perosis of choline deficiency was shown in Figure 4.7.

An enlargement of the hock joint, without slippage of the tendon of Achilles, has been shown to occur in young turkey poults deficient in niacin, biotin, vitamin E or zinc. Poults showing this typical enlargement at 3-4 weeks of age are presented in Figure 6.1. Although this enlargement of the hock apparently disappears during the 5-12 week growth period, it often returns in crippling severity after 14 weeks of age (Figure 6.2).

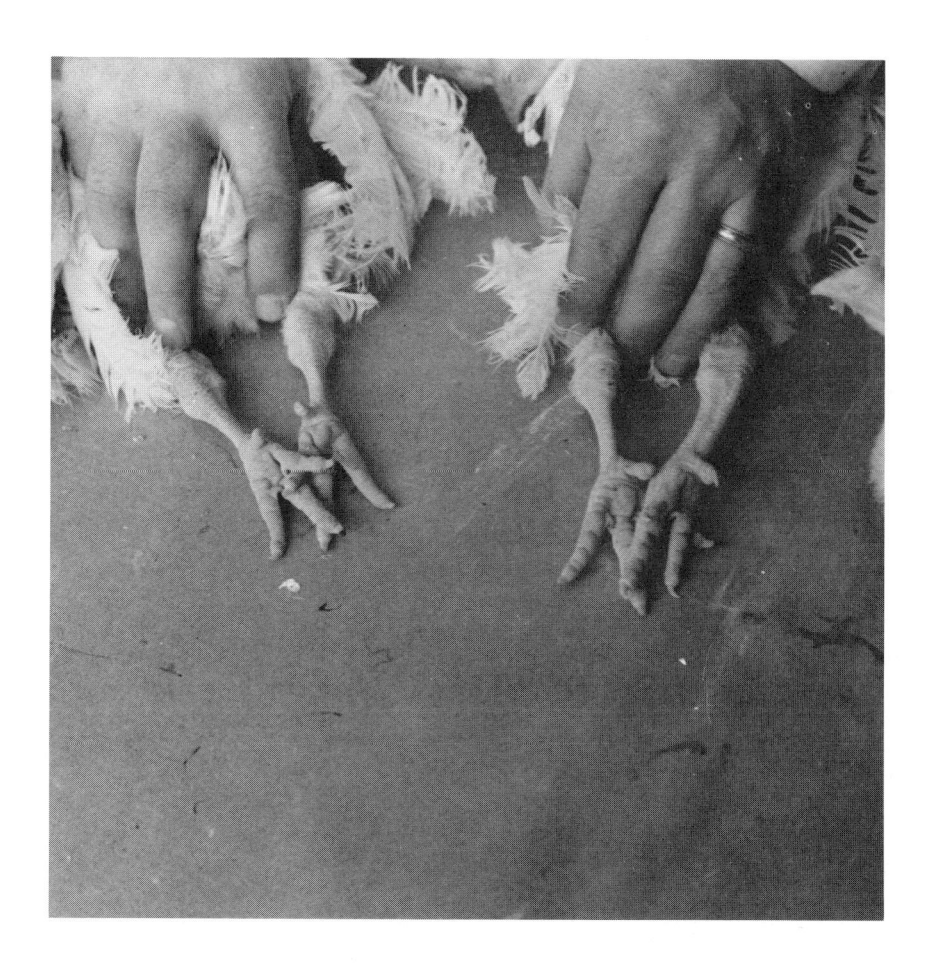

Figure 6.1 Poults showing typical early hock enlargements. This may occur with deficiencies on niacin, vitamin E, zinc, biotin, or an unknown factor present in brewer's dried yeast.

Figure 6.2 An adult turkey showing the result of "the enlarged hock disorder".

The requirements of turkeys for all of these nutrients, under normal commercial conditions, were discussed in Chapters 3 and 4.

Many phenomena, however, may create conditions that appear to bring about deficiencies of one or more of these known anti-leg weakness factors.

Among these are:

(1) Excess level of calcium in the diet. The excess, above that which can be absorbed in the duodenum, reprecipitates as flocculent, colloidal calcium phosphate having the capacity to adsorb manganese and zinc, and possibly other important nutrients, thereby causing a deficiency even in the presence of supposedly adequate dietary amounts of all required nutrients.

(2) Presence in the diet of rancidifying cod liver oil or other highly polyunsaturated fish oil (Scott, 1951). It is possible that such rancidity causes deficiencies of vitamin E and biotin.

(3) Use of moldy feeds or feeds in which the major ingredient (such as the corn) has undergone severe fungal fermentation. The author (unpublished) found that when the corn to be used in a poult diet was treated with about 20% by weight of water and allowed to stand over-night at room temperature, a yeast fermentation occurred. When this corn was dried and incorporated into a poult diet, most of the poults suffered leg weakness within two weeks, whereas poults receiving the same diet containing unfermented corn grew normally with no leg weakness. Analyses showed that the fermented corn had lost most of its vitamin E content.

Similar results were published by Sharby (1973) who found that poults receiving experimentally-molded corn showed severe leg deformities as early as 12 days of age. The molds used for the fermentations were *Aspergillus flavus* and *Fusarium moniliforme.* Poults receiving this fermented corn also developed air sac infections.

The special importance of biotin, and factors which may increase the biotin requirements of poults were reviewed by Scott (1968) and by Jensen (1969). Jensen and Martinson (1969) found the level of biotin needed to completely prevent the enlarged hock disorder to be in excess of 0.284 mg/kg diet. Kratzer, et al.(1958) emphasized that because of the special effect of phytic acid upon the zinc requirement, poults need at least 65 ppm of dietary zinc to prevent leg weakness.

Suggested levels of all nutrients that have been indicated to be concerned in prevention of leg weaknesses in turkeys are given in Table 6.1.

Unidentified factor in brewer's yeast

Although the incidence and severity of leg weaknesses in turkeys has been markedly reduced by the above discoveries over the past 35 years, some leg weakness continues to occur in well-managed flocks receiving diets that contain all of the above known anti-leg weakness vitamins, trace elements and amino acids in ample amounts. Under these conditions, addition to the diet of 2-3% dried brewer's yeast has been shown to prevent the weakness (Scott, 1951, 1953; Sherwood and Sloan, 1953; Hixson amd Rosner, 1954).

Additional evidence of an unknown factor in brewers' yeast was obtained in studies with chickens by Plavnik and Scott (1980) who found that broiler chickens reared on wire mesh floors in a very warm environment developed up to 50% leg weakness on a diet formulated to contain adequate levels of all of the factors given in Table 6.1 except for brewer's yeast. Addition of extra amounts of the vitamins, trace minerals and amino acids listed in Table 6.1 had no beneficial effect upon the leg weakness, but it was completely prevented by supplementing the diet with 2.5% dried brewer's yeast.

Early studies (Scott, 1951) indicated that the precursors of creatine (necessary for maximum muscle tone) might be needed in larger amounts than are sometimes present in certain practical rations. The studies showed quite marked improvements in the incidence of enlarged hock disorder when the diet was supplemented with 0.4% creatine. Addition of glycine and a source of methyl groups was found to produce an increase in the creatine content of the turkey muscles. Since glycine, arginine and methionine are the normal precursors of creatine in the body, it appears desirable to make certain that turkey rations contain plenty of these nutrients. Diets based on soybean meal are always adequate in arginine, but could be low in glycine and methionine.

In several investigations using purified diets containing a particular source of isolated soy protein (Dracket), the investigators reported a high incidence of leg deformity which was prevented when soybean meal replaced the isolated soy protein. Hunt, Baylock and McGinnis (1954) showed the problem to be due to the presence of sulfites in the isolated soy protein and the complete prevention of this leg weakness when the soy protein was washed free of sulfites before incorporation into the poult diets.

In retrospect, it is apparent that the early commercial-type rations with which a high incidence of losses from hock disorders occurred, were deficient in niacin, biotin and zinc. Addition to the diets of anything that improved intestinal microbial synthesis of niacin and biotin, such as the microbial growth factors, para-amino benzoic acid, inositol, certain antibiotics, and perhaps even distillers' dried solubles, caused improvements in the hock disorder through aiding in the synthesis of these required factors. Conversely, those substances such as lactose, intensified the problem by favoring the growth of heterotrophic microorganisms that competed with the host turkey for these nutrients.

Possibly, changes in the microflora of the gut helped in some instances to release niacin and/or biotin from bound forms present in certain feedstuffs, thus helping to prevent the hock disorders.

A further possibility of indirect action upon the hock disorder lies in the findings of Scott and Zeigler (1963) that certain ingredients, including distillers' dried solubles, appear to contain natural chelates that aid in the utilization of zinc.

Breast blisters

Development of breast blisters in market turkeys was a much more serious problem before the above discoveries were made concerning leg weakness than it is today. Much of the early breast blister problems of turkeys accompanied the leg weakness problem.

Other factors, however, also were responsible. Adams (1966) showed that the design of the wooden trough feeder being used was primarily responsible for the high incidence of breast blisters under the experimental conditions being used. He could not alter the breast blisters by changes in diet as long as the turkeys were being fed from a trough that allowed them to rest their breasts against and roost upon a horizontal board above the feeder. Adams found that these conditions, during the growing period, had much more to do with the occurrence of breast blisters than did wire floors or any other problem during the brooding period.

Studies with broilers in cages have demonstrated that the type of floor has much to do with the incidence of breast blisters. Any hard surface upon which the birds can rest appears to increase the probability of development of breast blisters.

A relationship between breast blisters and synovitis in turkeys was reported by Dobson (1966), who found that the incidence of both synovitis and breast blisters was much worse in confined turkeys than in turkeys on range. Furthermore, moving turkeys from confinement to range was accompanied by a reduction in both synovitis and breast blisters, while the incidence of both increased when turkeys were move back from range to confinement.

Pendulous crops

From time to time, turkeys have been found to develop a serious incidence of pendulous crops (Hinshaw and Asmundson, 1935; Rigdon, et al., 1960).

Early studies by Asmundson and Hinshaw (1938) demonstrated that the occurrence of pendulous crops is, at least in part, an inherited trait. It was reported that the tendency to develop pendulous crops under certain climatic conditions was determined by a recessive autosomal gene or genes.

Harper and Arscott (1962) reported that the feeding of a very high salt level (4%) during the period from 8 to 16 weeks of age, caused pendulous crops in both Beltsville Small White and Broad Breasted Bronze turkeys.

Usual cause of pendulous crops

When poults are fed a diet containing a readily fermented carbohydrate, particularly glucose, a yeast infection develops in the crop and the resulting carbon dioxide production causes such distention of the crop that food consumed does not readily pass from the crop to the proventriculus, thereby remaining in the crop to such an extent as to cause the development of a pendulous crop. This condition may develop in turkeys receiving practical rations that contain an ingredient such as molasses which supports yeast fermentation (Valarezo and Preston, 1974). It is possible to identify this condition by the "beer-like" odor of the breath of the poults. Nystatin, a fungal antibiotic, has been shown to have a beneficial effect upon mycoses of the crop (Yacowitz, et al., 1957).

Wheeler, et al. (1961) found that the organisms present in a pendulous crop destroyed many of the vitamins, particularly niacin. The extent to which niacin may be destroyed in the crop of turkeys not suffering from pendulous crops has not been investigated. Such destruction, if present, could contribute in some instances to the development of leg weakness.

Foot pad dermatitis

Serious open cracking of the bottom of the foot pad has been reported by many workers. This malady may have several different etiologies.

(1) Biotin deficiency has been demonstrated experimentally to cause both perosis and foot pad dermatitis in turkeys.

(2) Chavez and Kratzer (1974) reported a foot pad dermatitis that was not due to biotin deficiency. It occured in poults receiving a methionine-deficient diet containing soybean meal and

was prevented by adding methionine to the diet. Supplementing the diet with cystine did not prevent the condition, but appeared to aggravate it.

(3) Poorly processed or over-heated soybean meal has been implicated in this disorder. Apparently, poorly digested soybean meal causes sticky droppings that adhere to the feet and may cause the observed cracking (Jensen, et al., 1970).

(4) Abbott, Couch and Atkinson (1969) reported that the condition of the litter is all-important regardless of the type of soybean meal used in the diet. Foot pad dermatitis occured whenever the litter was damp or crusty; never with dry litter.

Tongue deformity

From time to time a peculiar tongue deformity characterized by a folding back of the tip of the tongue has been reported in poults. Several suggestions have been proposed as possible causes of this disorder.

(1) Because of earlier work indicating that a similar condition in chicks was due to a deficiency of the amino acid, isoleucine, Sanger et al. (1953) studied both chicks and poults fed isoleucine-deficient diets and reported the occurrence of the tongue deformity only during the time that the deficient diet was fed, and that the tongues became normal within nine days of feeding a complete diet. Returning chicks to the isoleucine-deficient diet brought on recurrence of the tongue deformity within 13 days.

(2) Bragg (1953) reported a low incidence of tongue deformity in newly hatched poults, and proposed that the condition is due either to a recessive genetic factor or to a genetic difference in nutritional requirements of the breeding turkeys. Bragg could find no evidence that deficiencies of isoleucine or any of the other amino acids were implicated in the disorder.

(3) In agreement with the experience of the author, Wright and Temperton (1955) reported that the primary cause of tongue deformity in growing turkeys under usual conditions is the feeding of an all-mash diet of very fine physical texture. In studies at Cornell University (unpublished) the author found that the presence of any appreciable amount of finely ground wheat in the mash of young poults produced impactions in the lower beak which caused the tongue to fold back, to become deformed and at times to slough off. Using cracked wheat or crumbling the diet prevented the problem.

Ascites

A severe, watery edema usually termed, ascites, has been reported to occur occasionally in growing turkeys. An early popular belief was that this condition was caused by the use of carbolineum, a tar-like product used to disinfect roosts, etc. The studies of Bressler, et al. (1950) showed that carbolineum did not have any such effect, but that ascites could be produced in high incidence by increasing the dietary salt level above 0.9%. Robblee and Clandinin (1961) found that high levels of sodium salts, either in the feed or in the drinking water, would cause the development of ascites. Morrison et al. (1973) also reported that high dietary salt levels increased the incidence of ascites, but they did not believe this to be the only cause of the disorder.

Selenium deficiency causes an edema, termed exudative diathesis. This disease is quite characteristic and also is accompanied by severe gizzard myopathy in young turkeys. It should not be confused with the type of ascites that is characterized by simple accumulation of colorless fluid under the skin.

Evidence exists that some types of ascites may be due to the presence in the diet of a "toxic fat" factor (Simpson, et al., 1959) or of certain toxic weed seeds or other contaminants in the feed (Scott, field observations).

Aortic rupture

Of all the peculiar anomalies of turkeys, one of the most interesting is the occasional development in adult turkeys of dissecting aneurysm of the aorta followed often by aortic rupture. This occurs, usually at about market time, often in some of the largest turkeys of well-managed flocks. It can present a considerable economic loss to the turkey producer.

Because of this loss, and because the turkey may represent a good "model" for the study of this malady which inflicts many deaths in humans each year, a large number of investigations have been conducted in an effort to determine the cause and treatments that may prevent dissecting aneurysms of the aorta in turkeys.

Wild turkeys are very high-strung, nervous animals. Even those hatched in incubators and reared in confinement, constantly pace back and forth in the pen, showing their instinctively nervous nature. Although domestic turkeys are usually docile, some happenings can arouse them to fever-pitch of excitement. For example, at sight of a hawk (or sometimes even a small airplane), turkeys on range may stampede to the fence causing trampling, injury and mortality among the flock. Some of these have been noted on autopsy to have died of ruptured aortas.

Following the report of O'Dell et al. (1961) that severe copper deficiency results in aortic ruptures in chickens, several studies were undertaken in an effort to determine if the aortic rupture in commercial turkeys was due to copper deficiency.

While Simpson et al. (1971) were able to produce aortic rupture in poults by feeding severly deficient diets, they did not observe any of this problem unless they added ascorbic acid to the copper-deficient diet. Little evidence has been obtained to implicate copper deficiency in the aortic rupture that occurs spontaneously in commercial flocks of turkeys. One problem in the study of this malady, is the low incidence of the problem in the field under normal conditions. Guenther and Carlson (1974) added copper as copper sulfate or copper oxide to a commercial-type turkey ration containing the usual, practical level of copper. Incidence of aortic rupture was very low among all treatments. Of the 200 Large White male turkeys on each treatment, only 4, 2, and 1 showed aortic ruptures with the basal diet, with copper oxide or copper sulfate, respectively. These differences were not considered to be significant.

In 1957, Barnett et al. found that the lathyrotoxic factor, beta-amino propionitrile (BAPN), at a level of only 0.1% of the diet, produced severe aortic ruptures in young poults. This was confirmed by many other workers. Although the condition resembled severe copper deficiency. addition of copper had no effect upon the aortas of turkeys receiving BAPN.

Treatment of young turkeys with diethylstilbesterol (DES) also was shown by several laboratories to induce an increased incidence of aortic rupture (Beall, et al, 1963). This also was not effected by the copper level of the diet.

Some evidence was obtained indicating that the turkeys prone to aortic rupture have higher blood pressures than those in which the disorder is rare. This finding led to many studies with reserpine and other tranquilizing drugs. None were demonstrated to have an effect upon the disorder (Speckman and Ringer,1961; Krista, et al., 1969; Simpson, 1974).

Simpson and Harms (1969) reported that the inclusion of oats, particularly dehulled oats, in the diet had a markedly beneficial effect upon the incidence of aortic ruptures in turkeys fed a diet high in animal fat. No effect of the oat feeding was found on blood pressure, total serum lipids or cholesterol.

Perhaps a critical finding was the discovery by Waibel and Pomeroy in 1957 that the feeding of 15% fish meal caused a 100% incidence of aortic rupture in turkeys receiving a low level (0.04%) of BAPN which in itself did not produce aortic ruptures. They showed the effect with six different samples of fish meal. All, at 15% of the diet, produced 100% incidence of the disorder. Fish oil was without effect. All of the toxic activity remained in the defatted fish meal.

Is it possible that the factor causing aortic rupture in turkeys is "gizzerosine", the substance shown by Okazaki and associates

(1983) to be responsible for producing severe gizzard erosions in broiler chickens similar to the "Black Vomit" that occurs in Peru among broilers fed fish meal in excess of 15% of the diets (Scott, 1985)?

Table 6.1 Suggested Nutrition for Prevention of Turkey Leg Weaknesses[1]

Factors	Amounts needed	
	Starter	Grower
Calcium, minimum, %	1.0	0.8
Calcium, maximum, %	1.4	0.9
Phosphorus, total, %	1.0	0.7
Phosphorus, available, %	0.8	0.55
Vitamin D_3, I.U./kg diet	3000	1800
Choline, mg/kg diet	2000	1750
Niacin, mg/kg diet	80	65
Zinc, mg/kg diet	75	65
Manganese, mg/kg diet	75	65
Biotin, mg/kg diet	0.3	0.25
Folic acid, mg/kg diet	1.0	1.0
Vitamin E, I.U./kg diet	30	20
Riboflavin, mg/kg diet	6	5
Pyridoxine, mg/kg diet	6	4.5
Ethoxyquin, mg/kg diet	110	110
Glycine, % of dietary protein	8	8
Methionine, % of dietary protein	2	2
Brewer's dried yeast, % of diet	2.5	1

[1] Recommendations are given approximately in order of importance of attention in practical rations.

In all instances, it is important to use healthy poults, free of *Micoplasma synoviae* or *gallicepticum.*

REFERENCES

Abbott, W. W., J. R. Couch and R. L. Atkinson 1969. The incidence of foot-pad dermatitis in young turkeys fed high levels of soybean meal. Poultry Sci. 48: 2186-2188.

Adams, A. W. 1966. The relationship of several factors to the incidence of breast blisters in large type male market turkeys. Diss. Abstract 26(9): 4923-4924.

Asmundson, V. S., and W. R. Hinshaw 1938. The inheritance of pendulous crop in turkeys (Meleagris gallopavo). Poultry Sci. 17: 276-285.

Barnett, B. D., H. R. Bird, J. J. Lalich and F. M. Strong. 1957. Toxicity of beta-aminopropionitrile for turkey poults. Proc. Soc. Exp. Biol. & Med. 94: 67-70.

Beall, C. W., C. F. Simpson, W. R. Pritchard and R. H. Harms 1963. Aortic rupture in turkeys induced by diethylstilbesterol. Proc. Soc. Exp. Biol. & Med. 113: 442-443.

Bigland, C. H. 1950. Ascites and oedema of brooded turkey poults in Alberta. Canad. J Comp. Med. 14: 144-156

Bonomi, A., and M. Langiotti 1965. The use of Nystatin in the feeding of turkeys. Soc. Ital. Sci. Vet. Atti. 19: 272-275.

Bowness, E. R., and J. E. Fahey 1954. Lameness in turkey poults. Canad. J. Comp. Med. 18: 335-337.

Bragg, D. D. 1953. An attempt to determine the cause of curled or deformed tongues in young Beltsville White turkeys. Poultry Sci. 32: 294-303.

Bressler, G. O., S. Gordeuk, Jr., E. W. Callenbach and G. H. Pritham 1951. The effect of salt and carbolineum in producing ascites in turkey poults. Poultry Sci. 30: 738-744.

Chavez, E., and F. H. Kratzer 1974. Effect of diet on foot pad dermatitis in poults. Poultry Sci. 53: 755-760.

Dobson, D. C. 1966. Influence of various management conditions on the incidence of breast blisters and Staphylcoccal synovitis in Large Type male turkeys grown both in confinement and on range. Poultry Sci. 45: 1080-1081.

Gries, C. L., and M. L. Scott 1972. The pathology of pyridoxine deficiency in chicks. J. Nutrition 102: 1259

Guenther, E., and C. W. Carlson 1974. Some effects of copper sulfate, copper oxide and 4-nitrophenylarsonic acid on aortic rupture and growth in turkeys. Poultry Sci. 53: 1931.

Harper, J. A., and G. H. Arscott 1962. Salt as a stress factor in relation to pendulous crop and aortic rupture in turkeys. Poultry Sci. 41: 497-499.

Higgins, W. A., J. B. Christiansen and C. H. Schroeder 1944. A Salmonella enteritidis infection associated with leg deformities in turkeys. Poultry Sci. 23: 340-341.

Hixson, O. F., and L. Rosner 1954. Effect of unidentified factors in yeast on growth and hock disorder of turkey poults. Poultry Sci. 33: 66-68.

Hunt, J. R., L. G. Blaylock and J. McGinnis 1954. Studies on a perosis-like condition in turkey poults. Poultry Sci. 33: 1061.

Jensen, L. S. 1969. Importance of biotin in practical turkey rations. Proc Distillers Feed Res. Counc. 24: 74-80.

Jensen, L. S., and R. Martinson 1969. Requirement of turkey poults for biotin and effect of deficiency on incidence of leg weakness in developing turkeys. Poultry Sci. 48: 222

Jensen, L. S., R. Martinson and G. Schumaier 1970. A foot pad dermatitis in turkey poults associated with soybean meal. Poultry Sci. 49: 76.

Jungherr, E. 1933. Staphylcoccal arthritis in turkeys. J. Am. Vet. Med. Assn. 84: 243-249.

Kratzer F. H., P. Vohra, J. B. Allred and P.N. Davis 1958. Effect of zinc upon growth and incidence of perosis in turkey poults. Proc. Soc. Exp. Biol. & Med. 98: 205-207.

Krista, L. M., P. E. Waibel, J. H. Sautter and R. N. Shoffner 1969. Aortic rupture, body weight and blood pressure in the turkey as influenced by strain. dietary fat, beta-aminopropionitrile fumarate and diethylstilbesterol. Poultry Sci. 48: 1954-1960.

Morrison, W. D. 1962. Growth and feed utilization of turkeys as affected by reserpine. Poultry Sci. 41: 1210-1213

O'Dell, B. L., B. C. Hardwick, G. Reynolds and J. E. Savage 1961. Connective tissue defect in the chick resulting from copper deficiency. Proc. Soc. Exp. Biol. & Med. 108: 402

Okazaki, T., T. Noguchi, Igarashi, Y. Sakagami, H. Sato, K. Mori, H. Naito, T. Masumura and M Sugahara 1983. Gizzerosine, a new toxic substance in fish meal, causes severe gizzard erosion in chicks. Agr. Biol. Chem. 47(12): 2949

Patterson, P. H., M. E. Cook, T. D. Crenshaw and M. L. Sunde 1986. Mechanical properties of the tibiotarsus of broilers and poults loaded with artificial weight and fed various dietary protein levels. Poultry Sci. 65: 1357-1364.

Pavcek, P. L., and G. M. Shull 1942. Inactivation of biotin by rancid fats. J. Biol. Chem. 146: 351

Plavnik, I., and M. L. Scott 1980. Effects of additional vitamins, minerals, or brewer's yeast upon leg weaknesses in broiler chickens. Poultry Sci. 59: 459

Rigdon, R. H., T. M. Ferguson and J. R. Couch 1960. Pendulous crops in turkeys-an anatomic and pathologic study. Am J. Vet. Res. 21: 979-986.

Robblee, A. R., and D. R. Clandinin 1961. The effect of levels of sodium salts in the feed and drinking water on the occurrence of ascites and edema in turkey poults. Canad. J. An. Sci. 41: 161-166.

Robblee, A. R. and D. R. Clandinin 1970. The role of biotin in the nutrition of turkey poults. Poultry Sci. 49: 976-981.

Sanger, V. L., D. M. Chamberlain, C. R. Cole, F. L. Docton and R. L. Farrell 1953. A disease of turkeys characterized by deformity of the tongue. J Am. Vet. Med. Assn. 122: 207-210.

Savage, J. E., D. W. Bird, G. Reynolds and B. L. O'Dell 1966. Comparison of copper deficiency and lathyrism in turkey poults.

J. Nutrition 88: 15-25.
Scott, M. L. 1950. Studies on the enlarged hock disorder (perosis) in turkeys. J. Nutrition 40: 611-624.
Scott, M. L. 1951. Studies on the enlarged hock disorder in turkeys. 2. Factors affecting the excretion and retention of creatine in young poults. Poultry Sci. 30: 839-845.
Scott, M. L. 1951. Studies on the enlarged hock disorder in turkeys. 3. Evidence of the detrimental effect of fish liver oil and the beneficial effect of dried brewers' yeast and other materials. Poultry Sci. 30: 846-855.
Scott, M. L. 1952. Effect of dried distillers' solubles, whey and lactose upon the enlarged hock disorder. Poultry Sci. 31: 175-176.
Scott, M. L. 1953. Prevention of enlarged hock disease in turkeys and ducks. World Poultry Sci. J. 9(2): 102-106.
Scott, M. L. 1953. Prevention of the enlarged hock disorder with niacin and vitamin E. Poultry Sci. 32: 670-677.
Scott, M. L. 1968. A review of the biotin requirements of turkeys. Proc. Dist. Feed Res. Counc. 23: 30-34.
Scott, M. L. 1985. Gizzard erosion. After fifty years of mystery, some answers. Animal Nutrition and Health 40(8): 22-29.
Scott, M. L., and G. F. Heuser 1954. Studies on leg weakness in turkeys, ducks and geese. 10th World Poultry Congr. 1: 255-258.
Scott, M. L., and T. R. Zeigler 1963. Evidence for natural chelates which aid in the utilization of zinc by chicks. J. Agr. Food Chem. 11: 123
Scrivner, L. H. 1946. Experimental edema and ascites in poults. J. Am. Vet. Med. Assn. 108: 27-32.
Sharby, T. F. 1973. Effect of feeding experimentally-molded corn to broiler chicks and turkey poults. Diss. Abstr. Int. 34: 1809.
Sherwood, D. H., and H. J. Sloan 1953. Studies with hock disorder in turkey poults Poultry Sci. 32: 923.
Simpson, C. F., and R. H. Harms 1964. Effect of diet on aortic ruptures in turkeys induced by dietary diethylstilbesterol. Poultry Sci. 43: 681-685.
Simpson, C. F., and R. H. Harms 1969. Influence of oat fractions on diethylstilbesterol-induced aortic ruptures of turkeys. Poultry Sci. 48: 1757-1761.
Simpson, C. F., R. H. Harms and J. M. Kling 1966. Relationship of dietary sodium chloride to aortic ruptures in turkeys induced by diethylstilbesterol. Proc. Soc. Exp. Biol & Med. 121: 633-634.
Simpson, C. F., W. R. Pritchard and R. H. Harms 1959. An endotheliosis in chickens and turkeys caused by an unidentified dietary factor. J. Am Vet. Med. Assn. 134: 410-416.
Simpson, C. F., J. M. Kling, R. C. Robbins and R. H. Harms 1968. Beta-aminopropionitrile-induced aortic ruptures in turkeys: Inhibition by reserpine and enhancement by monoamine oxidase inhibitors. J. Toxicol. Exptl. Pharmacol. 12: 48-59.

Speckman, E. W., and R. K. Ringer 1962. The influence of reserpine on plasma cholesterol, hemodynamics and arteriosclerotic lesions in the Broad Breasted Bronze turkey. Poultry Sci. 41: 40-45.

Stevens, V. I., R. Blair and R. E. Salmon 1984. Influence of maternal vitamin D-3 carry-over on kidney 25-hydroxyvitamin D-3-1-hydroxylase activity of poults. Poultry Sci. 63: 765-774.

Veltmann, J. R., Jr., and L. S. Jensen 1986. Vitamin A toxicosis in the chick and turkey poults. Poultry Sci. 65: 538-545.

Waibel, P. E., R. E. Burger and L. M. Krista 1962. Influence of reserpine and antibiotics on incidence of dissecting aneurysm in turkeys as induced by beta-aminopropionitrile. Poultry Sci. 41: 1554-1559.

Waibel, P. E., H. G. Lovelady and I. E. Liener 1964. Influence of beta-aminopropionitrile on dissecting aneurysm and on plasma amino acids in the turkey. Metabolism 13: 473-479.

Waibel, P. E., and B. S. Pomeroy 1959. Effect of diet on the development of beta-aminopropionitrile-induced vascular hemorrhage in turkeys. J. Nutrition 67: 275-288.

Valarezo, S., and T. R. Preston 1974. The effect of two molasses diets and a cereal diet on the pendulous crop condition in turkeys. Vet. Bul. 44(4): 247; Nutrition Abst. & Revs. 44: 797.

Wheeler, H. O., B. L. Reid, T. M. Ferguson and J. R. Couch 1961. Vitamin uptake studies on organisms isolated from crop contents of turkeys with pendulous crop. Poultry Sci. 40: 900-904.

Whitehead, C. C. 1984. Biotin intake and transfer to the egg and chick in broiler breeder hens housed on litter or in cages. Brit. Poultry Sci. 25: 287-292.

Wright, M. M., and H. Temperton 1955. Curled tongue in turkey poults. Vet. Rec. 67: 510-513.

Yacowitz, H., S. Wind, W. P. Jumbor, R. Semar and J. F. Pagano 1957. Use of Mycostatin for the prevention of laboratory cases of momoliasis in chicks. Poultry Sci. 36: 1171

CHAPTER 7

FEEDS AND FEEDING OF TURKEYS

The starting, growing and finishing rations shown in Tables 2.6-2.17 of Chapter 2 are typical of the types of diets used in much of the Eastern and Midwestern United States because corn and soybean meal are most plentiful, and will produce maximum results in turkeys at least cost of production.

In areas where corn is not readily available and therefore is more expensive than milo, milo-soy rations produce more economical results (as shown in Tables 2.21-2.32 of Chapter 2).

In some other areas, such as the Pacific Northwest, Canada, Australia, New Zealand and Great Britain, wheat is the most available and the most economical cereal for turkey feeding. In still other areas, such as Scandinavia, northern Germany, the Slavic countries and many others, barley may be the major cereal grain available for use at low cost. Asian countries may use considerable amouts of rice polishings.

Since a large portion of the research work in turkey nutrition has been conducted with "corn-soy" type diets, it is important to know the extent to which "alternative" feedstuffs can be used advantageously in rations for turkeys.

Nutrient composition of feedstuffs for turkeys

Studies that have been conducted on the energy values, on availability of protein, amino acids, and other nutrients have shown some differences between the utilization of some feedstuffs by turkeys, compared to their utilization by chickens. These differences have been small, however, and it appears, therefore, that the nutrient composition of poultry feedstuffs, as given in NUTRITION OF THE CHICKEN by Scott, Nesheim and Young (1982) can serve for calculation of the nutrient composition of rations for turkeys. Practical use of these values has proven this to be true.

Research on "alternate" cereal grains for turkeys

McGinnis (1983) has discussed the factors that must be considered in deciding to use "alternate" cereal grains in place of corn in rations for turkeys. Among these are:

1) Consistent availability and economical price.

2) Nutrient composition in relation to corn (i.e. protein, amino acids, metabolizable energy, linoleic acid, etc,).

3) Freedom from toxic factors (mycotoxins and others) that

affect turkeys.

4) Absence of enzyme inhibitors.

5) Absence of Beta-glucans.

6) Good digestiblity and availability of the proteins and carbohydrates.

7) Palatability and over-all acceptability to turkeys.

8) Freedom from dustiness, yet dense enough to flow well in manufacturing, transport and feeding equipment.

Good quality, No. 2 yellow corn possesses most of the good properties and few of the bad qualities listed above. It appears to be the most palatable and best accepted by turkeys of all cereals at all ages. Corn is highest in energy, and in linoleic acid. Good quality corn does not contain any detectable inhibitors or beta-glucans; it is highly digestible and therefore, does not cause loose droppings or other problems associated with loose, sticky dropping, such as foot pad dermatitis.

Most of the "alternative" cereals possess one or more qualities that limit their use. Even milo (sorghum grain) contains tannins that may be present in some samples at high enough levels to inhibit feed consumption and, thus, reduce growth or egg production. Milo also is lower in fat, metabolizable energy, methionine and linoleic acid than corn. These factors reduce its worth and must be taken into consideration when formulating least-cost, quality feeds for turkeys. In the early days of poultry keeping, no vitamin A supplements were used. Experiments conducted at that time showed corn to be vastly superior to milo and wheat. The reason for this was that corn contains enough cryptoxanthin, a well-utilized precursor of vitamin A, to supply the vitamin A needs of chickens and turkeys for normal growth, while no vitamin A precursors are present in milo or wheat. With the use of vitamin premixes to supply all of the vitamin needs, the presence of vitamin A activity in corn is of no value in determining its use against the use of milo or wheat in least-cost formulations.

Both the good and bad qualities of other alternative cereals will be discussed in the paragraphs below.

Wheat

Though not quite as acceptable as corn, good quality wheat is superior to milo and is being used as the major cereal in turkey diets with excellent results in many parts of the world. It's metabolizable energy content is almost equal to that of corn. The protein and amino acid content of various varieties of wheat vary considerably, running from about 10% (which already is better than most samples of corn), to as high as 18% protein, with a proportionate increase in amino acids. The usual protein content of "soft" wheat, grown in temperate climates, is approximately 10%. Some of the newly developed "cultivars" contain about 11% protein. The average protein in hard wheats is about 14%. Use of these higher-protein wheats is often economical because of the sparing effect that they exert upon the amount of soybean meal or other protein supplements needed (March and Biely, 1958).

Wheat has two major draw-backs compared to corn.

1) Wheat is relatively low in fat and, more importantly, in linoleic acid. This is less important in turkey feeds than in diets for chickens because turkeys appear to have a relatively lower linoleic acid requirement as percent of the diet.

2) Finely ground wheat may form a paste in the mouth of the poult and become deposited as a hard substance, filling the lower mandible such that there is no room for the tongue. This causes the tongue to curl back and become deformed. It may become necrotic and slough off. To avoid this problem, wheat used in poult feeds must either be cracked and screened to remove dusty flour from the feed; or the entire diet must be pelleted and crumbled.

Barley

Two types of barley have been studied in diets for turkeys. The superior type, containing about 12.5% protein and relatively less fiber, is grown in areas of plentiful water, either from rain or by irrigation. The second type is grown by "dry-farming" in arid regions. This type of barley is lower in protein and metabolizable energy and higher in fiber than the irrigated barley. While the irrigated barley is more useful than the arid grown barley both types are lower in energy than corn wheat and milo. Therefore, its use is limited and occurs only when barley is quite low in price compared to the cost of the other grains.

In most parts of the United States where barley is grown, the crop is harvested in the Spring--just before the onset of hot weather. Being a lower-energy ingredient, barley is useful for the purpose of lowering the energy content of the diet at the time when this is desirable because of the lower energy needs of the turkeys during hot weather. Barley also is higher in protein than corn and this helps in the summer when a little more protein is needed in the diet. At this time, therefore, it is often economical to use about 10-15% barley in growing and finishing rations for turkeys.

Barley does not serve well as the only cereal grain in the feed.

It is too low in energy; ground barley is too bulky to flow well in automatic equipment; and because of the sharp spears of hulls, it sometimes causes problems in the diet of young poults due to puncture of the gizzard. The latter problem probably does not occur unless the diet is one that produces gizzard erosions. Now that gizzerosine is known to be involved in gizzard erosion, the incidence of this problem should be almost eliminated (Okasaki, et al., 1983).

Western, dry-farmed barley has been shown repeatedly to be inferior to corn as the cereal portion of the ration for poults. Moran and McGinnis (1968) were able to improve the results with barley by 1) autoclaving; 2) addition of an enzyme prepared from a Bacillus subtilis fermentation; or 3) by addition of certain antibiotics to the diet. This was a culmination of a considerable amount of research at Washington State University on this subject (Fry, et al., 1958; Leong, et al., 1959).

The conclusions drawn from this work (Moran and McGinnis, 1965, 1966) are that barley, particularly dry-farmed barley, contains a relatively high amount of B-glucan which is indigestible by turkeys and chickens. This substance, if not altered by water-treatment, autoclaving or digestion with appropriate enzyme or enzymes, may bring about changes in the intestinal microflora which contribute toward diarrhea and sticky droppings with accompanying foot-pad dermatitis, and generally poorer health of the turkeys. Apparently, low levels of barley can be used without causing problems.

The use of 10-15% barley has been found to be beneficial, in many instances over and above its use as a simple diluent of the energy in corn rations. In areas where corn is not available and wheat is the cereal normally used, such as in Australia (Scott, unpublished, 1974), substitution of 10-15% barley for wheat appears to improve the acceptance of the feed by poultry, thereby resulting in improved growth and efficiency of feed utilization. Halbrook, Beekler and Smith (1954) showed, in experiments conducted over a three year period, that barley was more advantageous than oats as a supplement to "wheat" rations for turkeys.

Millet

Though usually not available for use in very large quantities at low cost, it is interesting to know that Goodearl and Moore (1941) obtained superior results when proso millet was used, wholly or in part, as a substitute for the corn in the turkey ration. Better growth was obtained in both males and females.

Triticale

This grain, which is an intergeneric cross between wheat and rye, is gaining favor as a nutritious grain for animal feeding.

Triticale grows well in temperate climates, often gives a higher yield per acre than wheat and has a higher protein content than most wheats. McGinnis (1973) reported that triticale in the diet of turkeys not only produced very satisfactory results, but also reduced the cost of the ration because its high protein content allowed for a large reduction in the amount of soybean meal needed as protein supplement.

CARBOHYDRATE SOURCES TO BE AVOIDED IN FEEDING TURKEYS.

Cassava (also known as Manioc, Yuca, or Tapioca)

An outbreak of severe, watery diarrhea in West Germany was traced to the use of cassava meal in the rations. Following the diarrhea, the turkeys became lame, and showed severe leg weakness by 17-20 weeks of age.

Cassava is known to contain the glucoside, linamarin. This substance, when acted upon by a certain enzyme, releases the very toxic prussic acid. Normally, the producers of cassava meal on a commercial scale are careful to wash the material sufficiently to remove this toxicity as measured in chickens. It appears possible that turkeys are susceptible to lower levels of this toxin. Perhaps they contain a higher level of the enzyme that releases prussic acid from linamarin.

Rye

Although triticale is quite well accepted by poultry, including turkeys, rye grain apparently is not. The use of high levels of rye in the diet of poultry has been shown to cause reduced growth and sticky droppings, indicating that it is not well digested. The "toxic" property of rye was found to be eliminated by water washing (Fernandez, et al., 1973) or by gamma-irradiation (Patel, Jami and McGinnis, 1980). McGinnis (1983) has suggested that the results indicate the presence in rye of a factor or factors that favor the establishment of deleterious microorganisms in the intestinal tract of turkeys. It may be possible to overcome this effect with antibiotics, thereby allowing rye to become the excellent feedstuff that its chemical analysis indicates that it should be.

ALTERNATE PROTEIN SOURCES

In many localized areas of the United States, and around the world, good properly heat-treated soybean meal is either not available or is too costly to use in comparison to the cost of alternative protein sources. It is important, therefore, to review the values and possible pit-falls in the use of alternative protein supplements.

Meat and bone meal

In those countries having a large livestock production, slaughter house wastes are quite plentiful and must be used to the best possible advantage. The products of the rendering of these waste materials are tallow, grease, poultry fat, blood meal, hog hair, poultry feathers and meat and bone meal. The meat and bone meal, usually having 50% protein, 10.5% calcium and 5% available phosphorus, is by far the major product of this industry, and the most important in rations for turkeys.

The fats and greases are very important and are used up to levels of about 6-7% in turkey growing and finishing diets to improve growth and, especially, feed conversions. The energy values of the various fats are given in NUTRITION OF THE CHICKEN.

Blood meal is rich in lysine but has a poorly-balanced amino acid pattern such that use of more than 2-3% blood meal is not advisable under most circumstances (Lockhart, et al., 1960). Kratzer and Green reported the available lysine content of spray-dried, soluble blood meal to be approximately 10-12%. Because much of the commercial blood meal is not of this superior quality, the available lysine level given by the NRC is only about 7% and Scott, Nesheim and Young estimate that the best level for use in feed formulation is about 6.7% available lysine in commercial blood meals.

Autoclave-hydrolyzed hog hair and feathers are useful as sources of cystine, but also should not be used at levels above 3-5% due to their poor balance of the other essential amino acids.

Meat and bone meal, even in areas where soybean meal is plentiful and low cost, has values in addition to its protein content that contribute to the balancing of a least-cost feed and to prevention of the enlarged hock disorder. The high level of available phosphorus, in itself is usually sufficient to call for the use of 8-10% or more meat and bone meal in turkey feeds.

For turkeys, meat and bone meal may have an additional value that is not so readily apparent. This is its relatively high glycine content. Scott (1950) conducted several experiments that demonstrated a need for a fairly high level of glycine together with a high level of choline for prevention of an enlarged hock disorder in young poults.

It appears likely that the young poult may not have developed an efficient metabolic synthesis of creatine, which is normally synthesized readily from glycine, arginine and a methylating agent. A reaction between glycine and arginine forms guanidoacetic acid the immediate precursor of creatine. Guanidoacetic acid must then be methylated to form creatine. This methylation is performed by S-adenosylmethionine which, upon giving up its methyl group can be reconstituted by a methylation from the betaine derived from choline.

Scott (1950,1951) found that supplementation of a basal diet with 1% creatine or with high levels of glycine and choline would reduce the incidence of enlarged hock disorder in poults at four weeks of age, from an average of 65% on the basal diet to zero.

Using graded levels of both choline and glycine, it was found that the optimum levels of these nutrients was approximately 0.2% choline and 1.8-2.25% glycine. This sets the glycine requirement for optimum growth and prevention of leg weakness in very young poults at 6-7% of the dietary protein (because the amino acid serine can spare the glycine requirement, the recommended glycine requirement for starting poults is given as 5.0% of the protein in Table 2.2)

In two separate experiments (Scott, 1950, 1951) it was found that supplementation of the basal diet containing 0.2% choline with 5% fish meal and 5% meat and bone meal reduced the incidence of the enlarged hock disorder in poults at four weeks of age to 0-10% from the high of 65% on the basal diet, and produced a growth response of 90 grams over the basal diet. The results indicated a need for additional creatine precursors. Further research is needed to pin-point the glycine-serine total requirement under present-day conditions, and to determine the extent to which present-day turkey feeds are meeting this requirement.

Meat and bone meal of good quality with consistent nutritional values, free of _Salmonella_ organisms is now available in most areas of the United States and other parts of the world. Poultry by-product meal, though having somewhat different nutritional values, is used also to provide many of the same nutrients as meat and bone meal, but to different degrees. A computer should be used to balance all diets when these ingredients are substituted for each other.

Fish meal

Before the discovery of vitamin B_{12} and before we had a good understanding of the critical needs for methionine and lysine in turkey nutrition, it was thought that fish meal was indispensible in all turkey starter, grower and breeder rations. Fish meal still is a very valuable ingredient for use in balancing diets with energy, methionine and lysine. It also contributes well toward meeting the phosphorus requirement and, perhaps most important of all, fish meal imparts a palatability to some otherwise poorly consumed feeds.

Fish meal is no longer considered to be indispensible. Excellent turkey feeds can be formulated to contain all of the factors needed for optimum growth and reproduction without the use of fish meal.

Because of its excellent nutritional values, however, the computer will bring fish meal into least-cost formulas whenever the price allows. Because of its effect on palatability, the use of 2-3% fish meal is desirable even when the price of it is slightly higher than its worth in least-cost formulations.

Rapeseed

Among the oilseed meals that have long been known to have ill effects on chickens and turkeys are two varieties of rapeseed. Because rapeseed grows in good yield in the cool climate of Canada, an immense amount of research has been conducted there to develop new, non-toxic genetic strains of rapeseed, and much research has gone into proving the non-toxicity and the nutritional values, particularly of a new cultivar of rapeseed known as Tower that has been given the trivial name, CANOLA. This cultivar, a Brassica napus variety, is low in both erucic acid and glucosinolate, the toxic substances present in high amounts in the original varieties. Clandinin and Robblee (1966, 1977) and others have reported that this rapeseed, when properly-processed, approaches the value of soybean meal, as long as it is used in a completely balanced turkey ration. Macgregor and Blakely (1964) reported that limited amounts of rapeseed can be substituted for soybean meal in turkey breeder rations without affecting egg production or hatchability. Many other protein supplements are available in various parts of the world. Some are excellent and can be used in large amount as long as the diets are balanced nutritionally. Others contain one or more factors having deleterious effects in turkeys. The amounts of these that can be used usually are determined on the farm by "trial and error".

BY-PRODUCTS OF WHEAT AND CORN MILLING

Wheat middlings, wheat millrun, wheat screenings and wheat bran

The by-products of the flour milling industry often are very useful in helping to reduce the cost of turkey feeds. These materials vary considerably in energy content. This must be taken into consideration in using them in turkey rations. Nevertheless, except for wheat bran, which finds much more practical use in ruminant feeds, the mill by-products often contain good nutritional values in relation to their cost.

Corn gluten meal and corn gluten feed

The by-products of corn starch and corn oil production are also useful at times in turkey rations. Corn gluten meal, because of its high xanthophyll content, finds its best use in broiler and layer feeds where yellow pigmentation is desired. Turkeys, fortunately, do not deposit much xanthophyll in the tissues and thus no call is made for highly pigmented turkeys. Corn gluten feed is higher in protein than wheat middlings, and often represents a useful ingredient in turkey rations.

FERMENTATION BY-PRODUCTS

Brewers'dried grains, corn distillers' dried grains with solubles, dried brewers' yeast and corn fermentation solubles

The value of dried brewers' yeast in the prevention of leg weakness was discussed at some length in Chapter 6. A level of 2.5% dried brewers' yeast has been found helpful in preventing an enlarged hock disorder in young poults.

Brewers' dried grains and corn distillers' grains are approximately equal in protein, but because of the higher fat content of the corn residue in the distillers grains, they are higher in energy and linoleic acid. Both often are valuable ingredients for use in turkey rations.

Corn fermentation solubles are less plentiful, but when available at low cost, may be used at relatively low levels.

PRINCIPLES OF FEEDS AND FEEDING OF TURKEYS

Several examples of least-cost corn-soy and least-cost milo-soy rations for turkeys of all ages were given in Chapter 2. As indicated above, many alternative feedstuffs are available in various parts of the world. These should be used, when economical, to provide the nutrient levels indicated as the requirements in the above-cited formulas and in other parts of this book. The best way to achieve optimum efficiency and economy of feed utilization is through feed formulation with the use of linear programming with an appropriate computer. The feeds must be formulated to contain all of the nutrients at the recommended levels indicated in this book, and thus be designed to produce top results in turkeys.

For the most part, we have dealt thus far with the growth rates, feed consumption, efficiencies of feed utilization, and nutrient requirements of large Broad-Breasted turkeys, grown to market weights at 16-18 weeks (hens) or 19-24 weeks (toms). This represents by far the majority of the turkeys grown in the USA and elsewhere.

Growth curves for these turkeys are given in Figure 7.1.

It is apparent that tom turkeys remain in the rapidly-growimg

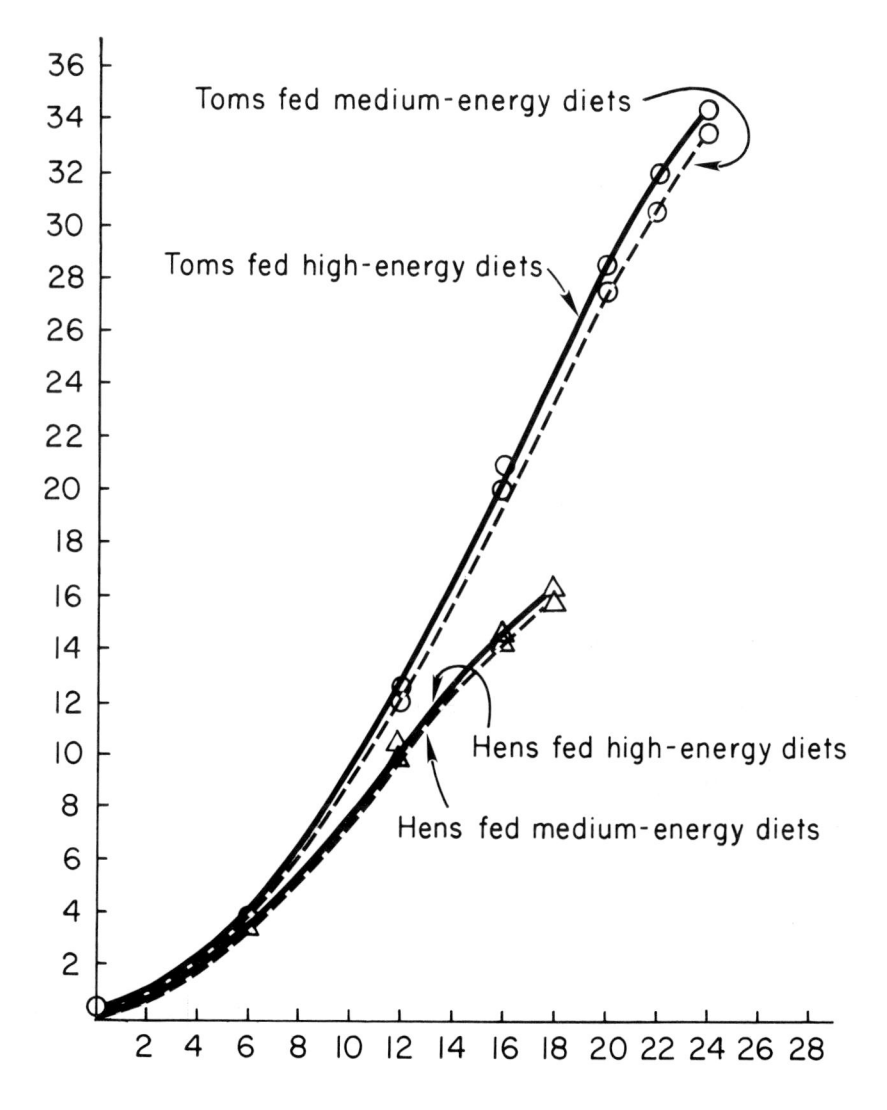

Figure 7.1 Normal growth curves for large Broad Breasted male and female turkeys.

phase until about 20 weeks of age. At this point, the growth curve breaks only slightly, indicating that toms could be carried to considerably larger weights if it were economical to do so.

As shown in Tables 2.3, 2.4, and 2.5, however, efficiency of feed utilization deteriorates rapidly after 20 mweeks in the toms. This is due to the high amount of feed required for maintenance in the very large birds such that relatively more and more feed is required for maintenance in relation to that used for growth.

Even so, it is being found economical in some instances to raise turkeys to larger weights for restaurants and institutional uses where a premium is warranted for these very large turkeys.

Efforts have been made at times to produce "broiler turkeys" by slaughtering the large-type turkeys at an early age--for example at 10-12 weeks of age. This has not been very successful for two reasons.

 1) The high cost of the turkey poult must be recovered in the sale of the finished product. If the poult cost was $ 1.20, for example, this represents a cost in the finished 12-pound "broiler turkey" of $ .10/ pound; whereas. if the turkey is grown to 34 pounds final weight, the poult-cost represents only $ .0353 per pound of final product.

 2) During the early growth phase, normal animals produce very little body fat. Thus the 10-12 week-old turkey resembles a "veal" animal with very little fat in the meat tissues. Since much of the desirable flavor is in the fat of an animal, these young turkeys are "dry" and not as tasty as are the mature turkeys that have accumulated sufficient body fat to be "juicy" and tasty.

It is possible to feed a finisher diet early--for example from 8 to 12 weeks of age, but growth rate will be much reduced and, also because of (1) above, this is not economical.

Thus, the best economy of turkey feeding usually lies in the use of rations that are least-cost for production of market turkeys, grown according to the growth curves shown in Figure 7.1.

REFERENCES

Clandinin, D. R., and A. R. Robblee 1966. Rapeseed meal for poultry-A review. World's Poultry Sci. J. 22 (3): 217-232.

Clandinin, D. R., and A. R. Robblee 1977.

Fernandez, R., E. Lucas and J. McGinnis 1973. Fractionation of a chick growth depressing factor from rye. Poultry Sci. 52: 2252-2259.

Fry, R. E., J. B. Allred, L. S. Jensen and J. McGinnis 1958. Influence of enzyme supplementation and water treatment on the nutritional value of different grains for poults. Poultry Sci. 37: 372-375.

Goodearl, G. P., and F. E. Moore 1941. Turkey feeding. N. Dak. Agr. Exp. Sta. Bul. 303: 1-22.

Halbrook, E. R., A. Beekler and E. P. Smith 1954. Turkey feeding research. Mont. Agr. Exp. Sta. Bul. 501: 1-14.

Kratzer, F. H., and N. Green 1957. The availability of lysine in blood meal for chicks and poults. Poultry Sci. 36: 562-565.

Leong, K. C., L. S. Jensen and J. McGinnis 1959. Improvement in utilization of barley by turkeys with a crystalline proteolytic enzyme. Poultry Sci. 38: 1221.

Lockhart, W. C., R. L. Bryant and B. W. Bolin 1960. Blood meal as a source of protein in turkey starting diets. Poultry Sci. 39: 720-728.

March, B. E., and J. Biely 1958. The sparing effect of wheat on the need for protein concentrates in a turkey starting ration. Canad. J. Anim. Sci. 38: 118-121.

McCuaig, L. W., J. M. Bell and T. F. Sharby 1977.

McGinnis, J. 1973. Nutritional value of some new and genetically modified cereal grains for poultry and feeding value of some alternate ingredients. Proc. 1973 Cornell Nutrition Conf. pp. 5-10.

McGinnis, J. 1983. Alternative cereal grains in poultry diets. Proc. 1983 Georgia Nutrition Conference, pp. 116-119.

Moran, E. T., and J. McGinnis 1965. The effect of cereal grain and energy level of the diet on the response of turkey poults to enzyme and antibiotic supplements. Poultry Sci. 44: 1253-1261.

Moran, E. T., and J. McGinnis 1966. A comparison of corn and barley for the developing turkey and the effect of antibiotic and enzyme supplementation. Poultry Sci. 45: 636-639.

Moran, E. T., and J. McGinnis 1968. Growth of chicks and turkey poults fed Western barley and corn grain-based rations. Effect of autoclaving on supplemental enzyme requirement and asymmetry of antibiotic response between grains. Poultry Sci. 47: 152-158.

Okazaki, T., T. Noguchi, I. Igarashi, Y. Sakagami, H. Sato, K Mori, H. Naito, T. Marsumura and M. Sugahara 1983. Gizzerosine, a new toxic substance in fish meal, causes severe gizzard erosion in chicks. Agr. Biol. Chem. 47(12): 2949.

Patel, M. B., M. S. Jami and J. McGinnis 1980. Effect of gamma irradiation, penicillin and/or pectic enzyme on growth depression and fecal stickiness caused by rye, citrus pectin and guar meal. Poultry Sci. 59: 2105-2110.

Scott, M. L. 1950. Studies on the enlarged hock disorder (perosis) in turkeys. J. Nutrition 40:611-624.

Scott, M. L. 1951. Studies on the enlarged hock disorder in turkeys. 2. Factors affecting the excretion and retention of creatine by young poults. Poultry Sci. 30: 839-845.

Scott, M. L., M. C. Nesheim and R. J. Young 1982. NUTRITION OF THE CHICKEN, 3rd Ed., M. L. Scott and Assoc., Publishers, P. O. Box 816 Ithaca, N. Y. 14851.

INDEX

Alternate protein sources
    Fish meal   168
    Meat and bone meal   167
    Rapeseed   169
Alternative cereals
    barley   164
    millet   165
    triticale   165
    wheat   163
Amino acid imbalances   33
Amino acid requirement
    breeders   74
    growing turkeys   30
    poults   32
Anatomy
    nutrition   9
Anoxia   93
Antibiotics
    aureomycin   141
    bacitracin   141
    oleandamycin   142
    penicillin   141
    tetracyclines   141
Aortic rupture   154
    copper deficiency   94
Arachidonic acid   137
Artificial insemination   17
    maximum fertility   19
Ascites   153
Barley   164
Beta-amino propionitrile (BAPN)   155
Beta-carotene   108
Biotin   123
Blackhead
    importance of control   16
Blood meal   167
Bone calcification   146
    potassium   92
Breast blisters   151
Breeders
    feeding of,   24
    rearing of,   19
Breeding programs
    objectives   15
Brewers' dried grains   170
Broad-breasted   14
Calcium
    absorption   9
    bone calcification   146

Calcium requirement
    breeders 88
    calculation 88
    poults 83
Canola 169
Cassava 166
Ceruloplasmin 94
Chloride deficiency 90
Chloride requirement
    breeders 90
    poults 90
Choline 128
Comparative feed costs 36
Copper deficiency 94
Copper toxicity 94
Corn distillers' grains 170
Corn fermentation solubles 170
Corn gluten feed 169
Corn gluten meal 169
Creatine
    synthesis 167
Cytochrome-c oxidase 93
Dicalcium phosphate
    anhydrous 87
    availability 87
Diet
    corn oil 138
    fish oil 138
Diethylstilbesterol (DES) 155
Diets
    formulation 33
Disease control
    management methods 16
DL-methionine 30
Dried brewers' yeast 170
Egg
    fatty acid composition 137
Energy requirement
    breeders 72
    poults 28
Energy:protein ratio 12, 24, 29
Enlarged hock disorder 168
Erucic acid 169
Essential fatty acids 137
Essential inorganic elements
    requirements 83
Exudative diathesis 96
Fat levels
    turkey diets 71
Fatty-acid-binding proteins (FABP) 71
Feather depigmentation
    iron deficiency 93

lysine deficiency   32
Feed restriction
    related to sexual maturity   19
Feed utilization   21, 33
    expected growth and efficiencies of,   36
Feedstuffs for turkeys
    nutrient composition   162
Fibrous feedstuffs
    utilization   28, 30
Fish meal   168
Folic acid   126
Foot pad dermatitis   152
Genetic selection
    improvements   14
    reproduction   15
Germ-free   141
Gizzard erosion   156
Gizzard myopathy
    selenium deficiency   96
Gizzerosine   155
Glucoside
    linamarin   166
Glucosinolate   169
Grass juice factor   142
    alfalfa   141
Growth curves   170
Growth responses
    3-nitro,4-hydroxyphenyl arsonic acid   141
    arsanilic acid   141
    aureomycin   141
    bacitracin   141
    copper sulfate   141
    penicillin   141
    tetracyclines   141
Growth resposes
    efficiency of feed utilization   21
Heat increment   71
History
    of nutrition   19
    of turkey nutrition   19, 22, 28
    origin of the turkey   7
Hock disorder   96
Hock disorders   95
Inorganic elements
    required   83
Iodine requirement
    poult   101
Iron deficiency   93
Iron requirement   93
Leg weakness   96
    disease   146
    genetic   146

177

    nutritional factors   146
Lighting
    colored lights   18
    light restriction   19
Linamarin   166
Linoleic acid
    requirement   137
Lysyl oxidase   93
Magnesium deficiency   93
Magnesium requirement
    poult   92
Management   8, 16
Manganese deficiency
    hock disorders   94
    poult   95
Manganese requirement
    poult   95
Manganese toxicity   95
Manioc   166
Meat and bone meal   167
Methionine hydroxy analog   30
Methionine-cystine requirement
    sparing effect by sulfate   30
Millet   165
Mineral requirements   83
Molybdenum requirement
    poult   102
Mortality
    causes   18
Mycotoxins and utilization of fat-soluble vitamins   116
Niacin   120
Nutrition   8
Nutritional muscular dystrophy   96
Omega-3 fatty acids   139
Pantothenic acid   121
Pendulous crops   152
Perosis   146
    choline deficiency   128
Phosphorus
    availability of, 85, 87
    bone calcification   146
Phosphorus requirement
    breeders   89
    poults   83
Physiology
    nutrition   9
Picolinic acid carboxylase   9
Potassium deficiency   92
Potassium requirement
    poult   91
Poults
    management   18

    rearing of, 18
Protein requirement 12
    breeders 72, 74
Protein requirements 28
Proventriculus 9
Prussic acid 166
Pyridoxine 125
Rapeseed 169
Riboflavin 119
Rickets 146
Rye 166
Scabby hip syndrome
    broilers, copper 102
Se-dependent glutathione peroxidase 101
Selenium deficiency
    poult 96
Selenium supplementation
    above requirement 101
Selenium toxicity
    poults 101
Selenomethionine 101
Silver toxicity 94
Sodium chloride
    dietary excess 91
Sodium deficiency 90
Sodium requirement
    hens, breeders 90
    poults 90
Starve-outs 18
Stress 91
Superoxide dismutase 93
Tapioca 166
Thiamin 117
Thyroid function 101
Tongue deformity 153
Triticale 165
Turkey
    breeds and varieties 14
    history of 7, 8
Turkey meat
    nutrient composition 13
    nutritive value 9
Unidentified factor
    brewer's yeast 150
    fish meal 139
    fish solubles 139
Vitamin A 108
Vitamin allowances 109
Vitamin B12 128
Vitamin D 110
Vitamin D3
    bone calcification 146

Vitamin E   114
Vitamin K   115
Wheat   163
Wheat bran   169
Wheat middlings   169
Wheat millrun   169
Wheat screenings   169
White turkeys   8
    development of Broad-Breasted   15
Xanthine oxidase   101
Yuca   166
Zinc deficiency
    poult   96
Zinc toxicity
    poult   96